Petrification and Progress

Petrification and Progress

Communist Leaders in Eastern Europe, 1956–1988

Olga A. Narkiewicz

St. Martin's Press
New York

All rights reserved. For information, write:
Scholarly and Reference Division,
St. Martin's Press, Inc., 175 Fifth Avenue,
New York, N.Y. 10010

First published in the United States of America in 1990

Printed in Great Britain

ISBN 0–312–05287–1

Library of Congress Cataloging-in-Publication Data

Narkiewicz, Olga A.
    Petrification and progress : Communist leaders in Eastern Europe,
1956–1988 / Olga A. Narkiewicz.
      p. cm.
    Includes bibliographical references and index.
    ISBN 0–312–05287–1
    1. Statesmen—Europe, Eastern—Biography. 2. Communists—Europe,
Eastern—Biography. 3. Europe, Eastern—Politics and
government—1945–1989. I. Title.
DJK31.N37   1990
947.084—dc20   90-41333
                                             CIP

Contents

Preface

As the twentieth century draws to its close, we are witnessing two interesting developments – the first being the dissolution of the two major blocs which have dominated the world, and most particularly Europe, since the end of the Second World War; and the second, a resurgence of interest in the past and a revival of interest in books dealing with recent history. These two facts, one tangible, the other less so, motivated me some years ago to document the history of the men who have governed the Soviet bloc since the death of Stalin. The book which resulted from my research dealt with the personal lives of several Soviet leaders, a topic inadequately covered by previous literature. Even the most important Soviet leaders such as Stalin had only merited two or three serious biographers; and the biographies tended to be political ones. In that case, what would future generations know about the less notorious leaders, men like Khrushchev, Brezhnev and Andropov? Though their tenure in office was shorter and their rule less dramatic than Stalin's, they introduced changes into the system which eventually brought to power Mikhail Gorbachev and the reforms which we have been witnessing in the late 1980s.

Some reviewers objected to this approach and criticised my departure from the schematic attitude of the political scientists; others, who understood the purpose better, praised it. Encouraged by this understanding, I realised that if the leaders of a superpower had had so little exposure of their private lives, the case was even more important when the leaders of the smaller East European countries were considered. The Zhivkovs, the Husaks and the Honeckers, who had influenced the policies in their respective countries for two or three decades, were barely known as human beings outside their own circle. In their own countries, they may have been considered heroes or villains; outside the Socialist Bloc, they were simply regarded as the puppets of the Kremlin, without a will or a personality of their own.

It seemed to me that there was a paradox in this situation. Almost all leaders have a strong personality; and in a totalitarian state (as the Socialist Bloc was characterised), personality matters more because the people have less influence over the rulers than is the case in a democracy. Hence, it seemed important to consider the lives of the leaders of the East European countries before they and their memory disappeared completely. This book is the result of this conclusion.

However, some problems arose in this connection. As I began to research and write it, it was clear that some changes were about to occur in the Socialist Bloc and its leadership, if only because of the age factor. But I did not anticipate that some changes would be so radical and so rapid as to surprise even the best informed world leaders. When the book was submitted in the autumn of 1989, it incorporated most of the events which had happened up to the month of October. But October and November of 1989 brought about an almost revolutionary situation. Hence, this preface will try to fill in some of the events which happened in these two months.

The Polish situation crystallised almost immediately, and caused few surprises. The new prime minister, Tadeusz Mazowiecki, chose to go to Rome to see the Pope on his first foreign trip, though it was later announced that he would arrange to see Mr Gorbachev in Moscow at a later date. Almost simultaneously it was announced that the West German chancellor, Helmut Kohl, would visit Poland and would grant the country a loan of US$1 billion to alleviate the most immediate hardship. This was to be a symbolic visit, intended to recognise the German guilt in having ruined the country in the Second World War. In the meantime, the Polish government decided to change the economy over to a capitalist one. Massive price rises for basic foodstuffs and energy were announced and it was planned to institute unemployment benefits for those workers who were made redundant as a result of rationalisation. The Catholic Church and the Polish Red Cross opened up soup kitchens, where apparently the need arose suddenly. According to some sources, the soup kitchen run by nuns in the Kielce region was greatly frequented, though the nuns made the recipient pray before being fed. The population as a whole waited sullenly to see the overall results of the changes, while Lech Walesa, the main perpetrator of the reforms, travelled to foreign countries asking for financial aid.

Hungary took a rather different path. The party and the state changed their names to conform with a 'democratic' image. East German refugees were being shipped to West Germany without any questions being asked, and free elections were being scheduled for early 1990. Hungary received its reward much sooner than Poland; on 26 October 1989 President Bush granted the country 'the most favoured nation' status in a ceremony held in the Rose Garden at the White House. In the welter of celebrations and memorial services for the victims of repression and revolution, the economic situation seemed strangely forgotten. Yet Hungary faces a massive foreign debt, galloping inflation and a serious feud with the neighbouring Romania. Whether the country will be able to negotiate these problems without a major upheaval remains to be seen.

While Poland and Hungary were proceeding with their reforms, perhaps going a little too fast and too far into uncharted waters, little seemed to be changing in East Germany, apart from the continuing flight of the population. It took the visit of President Gorbachev to celebrate the fortieth anniversary of the existence of the country for events to accelerate. As long as he was in power, Honecker refused to give way to the reformers. He spoke grimly about chaos and counter-revolution, and insisted that the country did not need any reforms. His deteriorating health and the Gorbachev visit changed the situation. Large crowds began to demonstrate in major German cities. The flight of the population continued on a larger scale than before. Finally, Honecker resigned on 18 October 1989, giving health grounds as his reason. He was replaced by Egon Krenz, who had been expected to become his successor. Krenz, who had been known as a hard-liner, surprised everybody by announcing drastic reforms almost immediately. His reforms did little to alleviate the situation; demonstrations, flight and new demands continued. Krenz went to Moscow for a briefing.

It was from Moscow, precisely at this moment, that the most

surprising developments came. In the last week of October 1989, a foreign ministry spokesperson announced that the Soviet Union would follow the Frank Sinatra doctrine, alluding to the crooner's song, 'I did it my way'. Another spokesperson announced that each country would be free to leave the Warsaw Pact organisation if it so wished. In other words, the Russians made it plain that they were following the Eurocommunist doctrine of a national road to socialism, except for the fact that they were also acknowledging that those countries may not choose socialism in the future.

Events in Germany escalated suddenly. In the first week of November the Politburo and the government resigned. Krenz announced the easing of restrictions on foreign travel and begged the East Germans to stay at home. They responsed by fleeing to West Germany. Finally, on 9 November 1989 the leadership announced that it was opening the borders and everybody could leave. Almost immediately crowds gathered at the Berlin Wall and started chipping away at it with hand tools. It was announced that eighteen gates would be opening in the Wall to make access easier. All that week the young Berliners celebrated, often holding parties on top of the Wall.

The euphoria was confined to Berlin. Chancellor Kohl cut short his important visit to Poland and returned to Germany to assess the situation. Amid the German joy and plans for reunification, the concerns of the American administration, the French and the British (not to mention the Poles), were muted but unmistakable. Only the Soviet government was expressing confidence that the outcome would be satisfactory and would result in the winding up of the NATO and Warsaw Pact organisations, and the creation of a 'common European home'.

A sudden meeting was arranged between President Bush and President Gorbachev on 2 December 1989, and was to be held on Soviet and American warships in the Mediterranean, off the coast of Malta. The American side insisted that the meeting had been planned for several months and that there was no agenda. The Soviet side stated that the meeting was called at a short notice and that the agenda would be the future of Europe. An observer might imagine three possible scenarios for the situation as it stands in November 1989. The first would envisage a cunning plot by the Russians to threaten Western Europe and the United States with a reunified Germany, destabilising all of Europe and reviving its revanchist dreams. The second would posit that there is a secret agreement between Kohl and Gorbachev that Germany would become unified and neutral in return for German economic and technological help for the USSR. Such an agreement has already been called 'Rapallo Two' even though it may not exist. The third, and possibly most likely, theory is that an over-impulsive Gorbachev, intent on his internal reforms in the Soviet Union, has allowed events to overtake him without realising the immediate consequences; namely the unleashing of the strong German pro-unification sentiments. He does not know East Germany well, and since it has for a long time been a showcase for socialism, he was unlikely to imagine the sudden display of discontent in the country.

If this last scenario is right, it is to be hoped that the American and Soviet presidents will find a quick and peaceable way to correct the European situation. If they do not do so – and the chances are that they will not – the future of Europe and the world may be at risk yet again.

Olga A. Narkiewicz
Vancouver, BC
November 1989

1

De-Stalinisation: The dilemma of East European leaders

The effects of the Stalinist legacy

From the moment that Eastern Europe and parts of Central Europe became integrated into the Socialist Bloc after 1945, its study was hampered by many factors. One of the main problems encountered is that we know both too much and too little about the countries concerned. We know too little because of the secretiveness which used to surround Communist governments (and often still does in the late 1980s); we know too much because Eastern Europe is still a part of Europe and because many scholars who work in the field are themselves of East European origin. As a result, the scholars in this field often set themselves impossible tasks and define unattainable objectives. One of the tasks relates to the question of the probability of Eastern Europe becoming a prosperous, democratic area after the end of the Second World War, had it not been incorporated in the Soviet sphere of influence. Another argument is developed around the question whether the socialist policies have blighted the East European economies to the point of no return. And there is also a basic, seminal question, which we are going to explore in this book: whether Eastern Europe has had the leadership it deserved, and whether the situation might have been different – and perhaps better – under more skilful leaders.

The work does not argue that Eastern Europe should never have become part of the Socialist Bloc. It takes for granted the fact that, for reasons which will not be explored here, this part of Europe was handed over to the USSR as a segment of a wider, global settlement, and that the Yalta Conference presented East Europeans with a *fait accompli* over which they had no control. But despite the acceptance of this fact, there are questions which can be dealt with. These hinge on the way in which the Soviet version of socialism was imposed and, much more importantly, question the kind of leadership which Eastern Europe had imposed on it since 1945, and, more recently, after de-Stalinisation.

There are many basic questions about the nature of leadership in Eastern Europe. One of the most fundamental ones is the fact that the leadership is not directly elected. The system relies on a series of indirect elections to produce the leader of the party. Due to the centralised system, the party leader is usually either a *de facto* or *de jure* leader of the government. Since, on average, only about 10 per cent of the population belong to the party, the other 90 per cent feel they are disenfranchised. Hence, there is an impression of undemocratic procedures and a perception of a leadership imposed from above by a small élite. Though this has been common knowledge for a long period, it has become evident that in view of the changing nature of the population, improved communications and the growth of technology, such unrepresentative government has become increasingly difficult to maintain. As a result, East European governments have suffered incremental difficulties in the decades following de-Stalinisation.

It has to be borne in mind that the practice of imposing a leadership has grown out of a hallowed revolutionary custom and it is not easy to jettison it. The early revolutionary doctrine of the 'dictatorship of the proletariat' appeared necessary when the revolution was in danger, while the clause about 'democratic centralism' was imposed on the Bolshevik Party in the perilous period of the Civil War. Though the practice has undergone certain modifications, it has never been totally eliminated. It is questionable whether it is – or should be – part of Marxist ideology; many Communists have maintained that it is not. Nevertheless it has been maintained for many decades, though it has not served well in those countries which became part of the Socialist Bloc after the Second World War. The irony is that even a minor show of democratic practice or of popular participation, which would not in any way diminish the power of the party or the government, might have satisfied the population. In fact, in several of the People's Republics minor democratic measures have been introduced since 1956, only to be immediately undermined by the bureaucracy or by the executive. As a result, such changes have been self-defeating and have, at best, produced discontent, at worst, major revolts.

It would be well, at this stage, to examine the reasons for such rigidity. An objective observer might conclude that the biggest obstacle to the setting up of democratic governments in Eastern Europe lies not only in Marxist dogma or in the centralised system, but is buried in past history. The past has intruded into the present to an extent which is difficult to estimate. Many roots of the problem lie in the vicissitudes which Communist parties faced between the wars and in the way in which the Comintern – the only authority over Communist parties abroad – disposed of the leaders. It must not be forgotten that in the 1930s, the main period during which Communist leaderships were being purged by Stalin, the majority of the newly installed leaders were inexperienced and untested. The German Communist Party provides the best example of this. It lost its leaders three times in less than two decades: first, owing to the early nationalist action; then through Stalin's intervention; and finally, in the Nazi purges. Other parties did not fare much better. After the Fascist take-over in Italy, most Italian leaders were either in prison or in exile, and substitutes had to be found quickly. The Spanish Communist Party lost its leadership in the Civil War and such leaders as remained spent almost half a century in exile. The Polish Communist Party was not only declared illegal by the Polish government in power in the 1920s and 1930s, but was also later decimated by Stalin's secret police. In general, in most Central, East and South-East European countries, Communist parties were illegal and persecuted for much of the inter-war period. The one exception was the Czechoslovak Communist Party, which was legal during this period, and only dismantled when the Nazis dismembered the country after the Munich agreement, when Czechoslovakia was divided into two German-dominated provinces.

It cannot be stated with any degree of certainty that the leaders who had been purged in the 1930s would have provided better leadership than their successors, particularly when their parties became ruling parties. But it must be borne in mind that their successors were not chosen for their outstanding leadership qualities; rather, they were carefully picked with a view to their personal loyalty to Stalin in the first place, and the CPSU (Communist Party of the Soviet Union) in the second place. Unconditional loyalty to a dictator is not a guarantee of good leadership. On the other hand, it does help to reassure the dictator that he is in charge.

At this point, one must enquire whether Stalin had any reason to fear independent Communist party leaders and why this strange and sinister episode of Communist purges ever took place. This must be done in order to provide a basis for the behavioural patterns of the new leaders. It has been maintained by many analysts that the purges were instituted without reason, though Stalin suspected that there was a conspiracy against him. Others have asserted that there was a plot against Stalin which originated during the early purges of the Old Bolsheviks (whose main support was in the Comintern), and which had, by the 1930s, reached the top commanders in the Red Army's High Command.[1] If the view of the former is accepted, Stalin would have to be classed as a dangerous psychopath, intent on ruining not only his country and the Communist movement, but also, in the final analysis, himself. This view does not square up with Stalin's behaviour in other fields during this period. While there is little doubt that he already suffered from some form of persecution mania in the 1930s, his (hypothetical) illness did not develop till late in life, possibly well after the end of the Second World War. The latter view – that there was an incipient plot – seems much more credible, when the events of the period are analysed.

According to information available at the time of writing, after the initial purges of Radek, Pyatakov and Sokolnikov, a conflict arose between Stalin and other members of the leadership, who were worried at the turn the purges were taking. A conspiracy is said to have been set up by senior officers, Tukhachevsky and his associates:

> The exact circumstances of Tukhachevsky's plot and of its collapse are not known. But all non-Stalinist versions concur in the following: the generals did indeed plan a *coup d'état.* . . . The main part of the *coup* was to be a palace revolt in the Kremlin, culminating in the assassination of Stalin. . . . Tukhachevsky was the moving spirit of the conspiracy.

The plot was allegedly discovered by the political police and Tukhachevsky was executed; his execution was announced on 12 June 1937. The writer who made these allegations had an intimate knowledge of all those concerned, which gave him some credibility, and he contended that these events forced Stalin to destroy anyone capable of forming an alternative government. 'Stalin could not be sure that avengers of his victims would not rise from the ranks of their followers.' As a result, thousands of military and civilian victims were purged. 'Refugee Communists from Nazi Germany, from Pilsudski's Poland, and Horthy's Hungary, who had in the past been connected with the one or the other faction or coterie in the Bolshevik party, were automatically caught in the net.' Whole leaderships were eliminated:

> Among the best-known foreign Communists who then perished were: Bela Kun, the leader of the Hungarian revolution in 1919, Remmele and Neumann, the most important Communist spokesmen in the Reichstag before Hitler, nearly all members of the Central Committee of the Polish Communist Party, and many others.[2]

Stalin's terror – whether there was some justification for it or not – weakened not only the Soviet administration and armed services; it also undermined most foreign Communist parties. Only the French and the Italian Communists escaped the purge; the former, possibly because they had a strong base in the country; the latter, because Mussolini had already decimated or imprisoned them before Stalin began the purges. The elimination of East European Communists did not stop with Stalinist purges. Soon afterwards, the Nazis occupied Eastern Europe and proceeded to eliminate such Communist leaders as were still left. As a result of these policies, the new leaderships, painfully constructed during and after the war, were untried and often mediocre, though there were some exceptions. The leaders who emerged after the Second World War generally belonged to one of two distinct categories: they were either Communists who had spent a long period of time in Moscow (for some of them exile lasted twenty-five years), and who had been spared during Stalin's purges; or they were underground resistance leaders in their own countries. The only feature which they all shared was that they had been chosen because they were believed to be personally loyal to Stalin.

When the war ended, the small Communist parties in Eastern

Europe (where, with the exception of Czechoslovakia, Communism had not been very popular) were further undermined by poor leadership. The insertion of large numbers of Soviet personnel into the leaderships of these countries – in the fields of secret police, military forces and administration – eroded the parties' strength further and circumscribed the limited amount of independence which their leaders might have had *vis-à-vis* their large neighbour. Indeed, the leaders' powers were almost entirely illusory; with one exception, that of Yugoslavia, they had little chance of staying in government without the presence of the Soviet armies. This situation created a vicious circlȩ: as long as the leaders had little or no power, apart from that granted by the Soviet occupiers, the leadership posts would not attract gifted personalities. And as long as the mediocre leaders were in top posts, there was little chance of improving the state apparatus, the economy and the self-esteem of the nation. This state of affairs prevailed throughout Eastern Europe till the death of Stalin, and lingered on to some extent for several decades after de-Stalinisation.

The leadership in 1956

Given the poor calibre of the East European leaderships, it is hardly surprising to find that Khrushchev's Twentieth Congress speech in 1956 created so many problems in the Bloc. Rather, it is surprising that the problems were relatively limited and that they were overcome within a short period of time. The problems arose because, for the first time since Communist governments were introduced, the population of the Bloc was suddenly released from the tyranny of Stalinism and was able to express its opinions at last, even if only for a short while. It seemed only natural that the first demands would be for the removal of the inept and corrupt Stalinist leaders.

In some instances, removals were effected; in other cases, the governing leaders improved their practice of government. But the legacy of Stalinism remained. It would be negligent to ignore the legacy that the post-Stalinist leaders had inherited: one of scarcity of commodities, abuses of power, blatant cruelty and purges. Such characteristics are not easily forgotten. The persecution of opponents in the Stalinist period has been compared to the persecution of suspected heretics in the Middle Ages. One of the accused in the medieval period confessed to being a disciple of Satan, in which capacity he and his companions purported to have destroyed the Frankish kingdom, including its wine, corn and fruits. A commentator noted:

Who can fail to recognize the confession of a 'Trotskyite monster' or a 'Judeo-Titoist'. Everything is there, . . . the sudden promotion to the rank of qualified saboteur, the abject submission to the order of a Satanic, Trotskyite, Titoist or other center, and even moralizing intentions.

It was this climate of fear, repression and medieval-style trials that created many of the difficulties for the post-Stalinist leaderships. Too much blood had been spilt in the eager pursuit of heretics; too many ghosts haunted the corridors of power. It was difficult to forget so much suffering, bitterness and fear, and to pretend that normalcy could be restored with one speech. Few believed the rationalising efforts to justify the trials:

All the difficulties which emerged in the new attempts to 'build socialism', all the evils which weakened the satellites, were now explained and justified by the secret activity of the diabolical bands of Rajks, Kostovs . . . and the rest, the servants of Judas Tito, who was himself a servant of Satan Truman.[3]

The return to rational thinking after Khrushchev's denunciation of Stalin's crimes only served to increase the bitterness. If all those accused had died in vain, what chance was there for the new leaders? Would another Stalin rise at some point and repeat the same crimes?

It was in this climate of anger and disillusionment that the East European leaders had to govern after 1956, and to try to undo the worst effects of Stalinism, while at the same time, they were prevented from introducing pluralism into a monolithic system. In general, their efforts were not very successful. Though one of Khrushchev's aims in making his speech had been to reassure everyone that Stalinism could never recur, not many believed him. Because of this, many leaderships refused to introduce any changes; while some nations, emboldened by the 'thaw', took the law into their own hands and overthrew their governments. Khrushchev himself was neither sufficiently secure in his post nor sufficiently well-informed to impose gradual changes in the Bloc; he could only react to events as they occurred. Thus, when dramatic changes occurred in Poland, where the Stalinist leadership was ousted despite Soviet protests, there were immediate Soviet threats of military retaliation. This retaliation was only prevented when the new Polish leadership assured the Russians that socialist policies would be continued. In Hungary, where the leadership wanted to reverse almost all socialist measures, such compromise proved impossible. The Hungarian revolution was quelled by Soviet troops. But there were also countries which were almost untouched by the invitation to de-Stalinise.

In some East European countries, the Stalinist leaders stayed in power and even enjoyed Khrushchev's patronage. In Czechoslovakia, Antonin Novotny, the successor to Gottwald, who had died in 1953 and as Stalinist as his predecessor, became First Secretary of the Party with Khrushchev's support, after the latter had attained this post in the Soviet Union. In Romania, Gheorgiu Dej appeared to loosen his grip on the country and even announced some concessions to farmers and consumers; but his political attitudes did not change, nor did he step down in favour of a non-Stalinist. In Bulgaria, the Stalinist Chervenkov announced that the cult of personality was dead and ordered the removal of his portraits from public places; but he did not resign, though he appointed Todor Zhivkov as First Secretary. The then little-known Zhivkov was later to take over Chervenkov's posts and continue the same ideological policies. In Albania, still within the Soviet sphere of influence (though not for much longer), Enver Hoxha held on to the leadership and did not change his course. And there was no change of leadership in East Germany, where Ulbricht survived the Berlin workers' uprising of 1953, as well as an attempt to depose him by his subordinates, continuing to implement Stalinist policies till he had to step down owing to advanced age.[4]

In effect, therefore, the leadership was radically changed in only two countries; in others, governments introduced a few cosmetic changes. However, where the former leaders remained in place, they soon found that they were virtually on probation. In view of the fact that the Soviet leadership was pressing for radical change and the liberalisation of the systems, in keeping with the liberalisation in the Soviet Union, this was rather surprising. Since the old leaders were not prepared to implement radical changes, it would be natural to assume that they would have been removed from office. Two explanations can be proffered for this: either those leaders had far more support in their countries than is generally acknowledged, or the Soviet leadership had far less power than is assumed.

This work will examine the first hypothesis when individual leaders are discussed; the second hypothesis need hardly be considered. When the Soviet leadership really wants to effect a change, it does so, even if this requires military intervention. The examples of Hungary in 1956, Czechoslovakia in 1968, Afghanistan in 1979 and Poland in 1981 show that the pattern is well established and effective. For the purposes of this enquiry, it is irrelevant to investigate whether such changes are first demanded by the military and carried out by the Party, or whether the reverse is the case. It is sufficient to note that such interventions are carried out when the perceived threat to national security is considered too dangerous to ignore. On balance, it can be stated with certainty that if the Stalinist leaders in the East European Bloc had been considered unsound, they would have been removed within a short period of time. The conclusion, therefore, must be that the leaders who remained in power were thought to be too valuable for Soviet interests to be ousted – either because of their overwhelming loyalty to the CPSU, or because of their ability to maintain order in their respective countries.

By the same token, though, the Stalinist leaders had a difficult task ahead of them. On the one hand, and at the very least, they had to make a show of liberalisation in order to placate the Soviet leadership; on the other hand, they had to maintain order and stability in an unstable and volatile situation. All of Eastern Europe had been shaken and shocked by the developments at the Twentieth Congress of the CPSU, the subsequent change of power in Poland and the Hungarian revolution. The leaders, both old and new, were forced to remove the main points of friction while, simultaneously, they had to try to maintain their own power and influence. It is surprising to find that some of them actually succeeded in this apparently impossible task.

The problems facing East European leaderships will only be touched upon briefly here, but it is necessary to outline the most important ones. The foremost of these was the removal of the Stalinist machinery of terror, which had been so powerful that it took precedence over almost all the other affairs of the state. This was only partially accomplished. In Hungary, after the dismantling of the secret police during the uprising, a wave of terror was instituted when the revolution was over, in order to hunt down all the revolutionaries who were still alive and in the country. After a period of time, Janos Kadar, always pragmatic, reversed the policy of terror and introduced some liberalisation. All those revolutionaries who had not taken a leading part in the events were allowed to return to their former posts. The leaders of the revolution, however, were not so fortunate.

Imre Nagy, the leader of the revolutionary government, who had been held prisoner since 1956, was finally executed with three other revolutionaries in June 1958. Kadar disclaimed responsibility for these executions, and it was mooted that the Hungarians were executed because of Khrushchev's fear of Yugoslav 'revisionism'; it was also claimed that the Chinese insisted that those who had sponsored the revolution must be punished. It is quite true that Khrushchev condemned the Yugoslav role in the Hungarian uprising:

> In his Sofia speech Khrushchev publicly condemned Yugoslavia's role
> in the Hungarian uprising. During the 'counter-revolutionary *putsch*'
> of 1956 . . . the Yugoslav embassy in Budapest 'had become the
> centre for those who were struggling against the Popular Democratic
> regime', and then 'the place of refuge for the treacherous,
> capitulationist Imre Nagy – Losonczi group.' From that moment it
> looked as though Imre Nagy's fate was sealed. . . . Everything
> indicated that the decision to put him on trial and execute him, in
> spite of Kadar's pledges to the contrary in 1956, was taken, not in
> Budapest . . . but at an international level, perhaps at the Warsaw
> Pact meeting in Moscow at the end of May.

The reason for this may have been that, at this stage, relations with Yugoslavia deteriorated and Khrushchev 'no longer had the will or the desire to protect the man whom he had himself helped to bring to power.'[5]

While the leaders of the Hungarian uprising were finally sacrificed because of pressure from some quarters (and, more than thirty years later, it was still unclear where that pressure came from), the minor actors in the Hungarian drama were either pardoned or released from prison after serving part of their sentences, and were allowed to carry on with their work. In due course, Kadar's policy of liberalisation had virtually dismantled most of the machinery of terror, and this made Hungary one of the most liberal countries in the Bloc.

Poland did not have such a smooth passage towards liberalisation. Although political prisoners were released in 1956 and many citizens were allowed to leave the country, the secret police kept its considerable powers of surveillance, if not its powers of summary arrest and questioning. On coming to power, Gomulka had promised that the hundreds of thousands of files, which the secret police kept on those suspected of dissidence, would be destroyed. In fact, there was a strong suspicion that the files were merely moved from the building in which they had been stored to another location. However, the overt terror machine was relaxed and would only be used in moments of major disturbances, or against the most vocal opponents of the government.

Little was done to ease police powers immediately in other countries, although some relaxation was achieved at a later stage in East Germany. In Romania, Bulgaria and Czechoslovakia, the leadership either failed to relax police powers or to liberalise the political climate. But gradually the Communist leaders who had been tried in show trials and executed would be rehabilitated. Such piecemeal actions did little or nothing to reconcile the population to the continued rule of the same leaders who had initiated the purges. In one case, that of Czechoslovakia, this petrification of the government led directly to the events of 1968. While nothing of the kind occurred in Romania and Bulgaria, the reason for this lay more in the specific conditions in those countries than in any degree of liberalisation.

Liberalisation apart, the great mass of the population was most interested in the rise of the standard of living. Hungary enjoyed massive Soviet subsidies after the revolution, in order to pacify the population, and the standard of living rose. Poland managed to obtain some economic help and bank loans from the West, and the shortages decreased. Other countries in the Bloc did not fare so well. East Germany developed a new economic plan, based on its large scientific and technological potential, but it took some years to implement it. Bulgaria stagnated for a decade, still a backward, agricultural economy. Romania embarked on an ill-conceived and over-hasty industrialisation. And Czechoslovakia, previously the industrial miracle of the Eastern Bloc, froze under its Stalinist leadership. Serious economic problems developed and the standard of living slipped to some degree.[6]

It can be seen from the above that the record was uneven and produced mixed results. However, some minor improvements were made and these allowed the leaderships some breathing space in which to plan major reforms. In most cases, though, these reforms were either not carried out, or, where implemented, were not successful enough to satisfy the population. Even more importantly, they failed to effect the overdue modernisation of Eastern Europe. At a later stage, all the leaderships were to acknowledge this and would try to remedy the position. But by then so many things had gone wrong that partial tinkering with reform only made matters worse.

Like the elimination of terror, the economic reforms were undertaken in a half-hearted fashion which did not promise much for the future. Attempts at reforms in other spheres also created problems. The restoration of intellectual freedom was a telling case. The leaders were adamant that the system they called socialist was not to be radically changed (they had to insist on this, since their continued existence in power depended upon it), but even with this proviso, there was little reason why intellectual freedom should not be allowed to flourish. A return to a free exchange of ideas was particularly important in view of the fact that East European science, technology and social science had lagged behind the rest of the world during the Stalinist period. This backwardness, along with other obstacles, impeded the Bloc's economic and technological growth.

In general, the leaderships refused to face the dilemma directly. It was admitted that intellectual freedom was important, but intellectuals were still greatly mistrusted, because they were considered to be the most likely elements to lead the rest of the population in political dissent. Moreover, the intellectuals needed contacts with foreign intellectuals. It followed that freedom to travel abroad and to exchange ideas would have to be condoned, if not actually encouraged. Once again, the response of the leaderships was uneven and unenthusiastic. The Polish government allowed the intellectuals to travel abroad freely, provided they did not voice strong anti-government sentiments. Hungarian intellectals had to wait for this freedom much longer, but were eventually allowed to travel when and where they wished. But the Czechs and the Bulgarians were not permitted to travel abroad, and the Romanians were subject to so many draconian rules that they were virtually cut off both from the West and the Eastern Bloc for a long time. In East Germany, the situation deteriorated after the building of the Berlin Wall and for a lengthy period the East Germans were almost sealed off from foreign contacts.

Hence, the position was not normalised and much depended on the favour of officials in charge of passport offices. If such was the position in cases where foreign contacts were deemed necessary, the lot of ordinary citizens was much worse. Once again, the leaderships failed to give a clear lead in a matter of great importance to many citizens. Though bottlenecks could have been expected, the erratic fashion in which passports were granted or withheld aggravated an unpleasant situation into an explosive issue. Charges of favouritism could be levelled at many officials, and this created additional hostility between the apparatus and the ordinary citizen.

However, travel to the West was only part of the problem. There were also many obstacles to travel within the Bloc, and serious difficulties were encountered travelling to the Soviet Union. It would appear that the East European leaderships had no intention of allowing too much free travel outside the borders of their own countries, and since travel abroad conferred certain privileges (such as the possibility of acquiring hard currency), the limitations produced even more irritation.

Although an observer may be tempted to blame all the above listed difficulties on the obtuse and devious policies pursued by the leaderships, it is certain that many of them were merely due to bureaucratic practice. Nevertheless, they helped to maintain a climate of lack of confidence in the leaderships and provided further proof of their inconsistency. Indeed, it is difficult to assess why the leaderships did not remedy such situations, although one can offer some explanations. It may be that the leaders either did not see the grievances, or did not understand them. Further, they may have been constrained by external pressure to concede as little as possible to the population at large. And, finally, they may have been so immersed in their own problems – which were manifold – that they had little time to spare for the problems of the population.

Such disregard for the new and more relaxed atmosphere in the post-Stalinist era seemed to prove that the leaders were not capable of fulfilling their obligations. And, indeed, while some of the leaders relaxed somewhat, and others paid lip-service to relaxation, it appeared to many that none of them grasped the essence of the change. If this were the case, then it seemed obvious that the leaders were incapable of governing.

Personalities in power in 1956

At this stage, the leaders in power in the Bloc faced considerable difficulties. Those remaining in office, despite their Stalinist past, had to make strenuous efforts to retain power, while at the same time being forced to make sufficiently reformist gestures to convince everybody that they had changed their course, even though they had little intention of implementing reforms. The newly installed leaders were in an even more difficult position. They had either been carried to the top on a wave of popular enthusiasm or were appointed for want of better candidates. They were new to their posts, often had little or no experience of the higher reaches of goverment, and they could not rely on their subordinates to carry out their policies. As a result, directives were often insufficient or contradictory and their implementation (if carried out), usually faulty. In sum, it can be stated with some certainty that the leadership in 1956 was both confused and inadequate. Much of the reason for this lay in the personal make-up of the leaders themselves.

It has already been stated at the outset, but cannot be repeated too often, that the leaders in the Socialist Bloc do not attain their posts as a result of general elections. Because of the hierarchical nature of the appointments, they do not undergo the strenuous round of electoral tours which test politicians in parliamentary democracies. It is quite true that the socialist leaders have to lobby for support within their own party and have to be approved by the CPSU, but that process is not comparable to a parliamentary electoral process. Because of this, even if the leaders happen to be genuinely popular in their own country, the general perception is that they have been imposed, rather than elected. This lack of choice (even if the choice is only illusory) makes the leaders easy targets for criticism, for the population at large does not feel as though it had participated in their election. Although most East European countries have had little or no experience of parliamentary democracy in the past, they are, both by tradition and temperament, more inclined to political pluralism than to monolithic government.

Stalinism was a great equaliser; under duress the Eastern Europeans accepted the imposed leaderships as an evil which could not be avoided and too dangerous to challenge. When Stalinism was declared to be over, the population expected more than a slight relaxation of the former regime; at the very least, it wanted some form of electoral choice. The reformed socialist system did not allow for this, and the leaders were unable (or unwilling) to change it radically. The main reason for this lay not only in external pressures, but in the manner of their own accession to power. A brief review will demonstrate why each leader had strong reasons to cling to power as long as possible.

While not all leaders had the same blood-stained records, some of them had well-founded fears of retribution from within their own party, if not their country. Bulgaria had a particularly troubled history of leadership succession. Chervenkov, a hardline Stalinist, resigned in favour of the young Todor Zhivkov, though he shared the posts of prime minister and first secretary with him for a few years. Finally Zhivkov managed to oust Chervenkov completely. He proceeded to rehabilitate the executed Kostov, but limited liberalisation to very few measures. Though Zhivkov was young on his accession to power, he could in no way have been considered a liberal. However, he did enjoy the support of Nikita Khrushchev, and he was flexible enough to experiment with economic reforms.

Other countries fared rather worse. In Czechoslovakia, Antonin Novotny, a survivor of the Stalinist purges, stayed in power. To prove his changed policies, he announced in March 1956 that the party attached particular importance to co-operation with Yugoslavia. Co-operation with Yugoslavia was, in those early days, considered to be equivalent to liberalisation. But despite such announcements little was done in reality, though it must be added that the Yugoslav model was not necessarily suited to Czechoslovak conditions of the time.

In East Germany, Ulbricht continued to govern as before and even began to press Khrushchev to stop the current wave of enthusiasm for the Yugoslav experiment. Soon it became apparent that the Yugoslav model was beginning to worry Khrushchev himself, and he became more than ready to listen to the views of Ulbricht, Novotny and the French party leader, Maurice Thorez, rather than listen to Tito and his associates. The German leadership in particular prided itself on the fact that there had been no 'traitors' in the party: 'In fact, our party's general line has always been correct. There have been no Rajk or Kostov trials here; such errors are not relevant in our case,' said *Neues Deutschland* on 29 April 1956. Nevertheless, the government released Franz Dahlem, who had been involved in the Slansky trial, as well as eighty other Communists, seven hundred Social Democrats and some twelve thousand other political prisoners. 'That was as far as de-Stalinization went,' commented one writer. The East German party and government were to retain their sanctimonious attitude throughout this period, but many reforms were introduced in a covert manner. The authorities' main effort was aimed at raising the standard of living of the nation, at increasing the productivity of industry and at making their country the technological flagship of the Bloc. In all these undertakings they were remarkably successful, and this may have been the reason why East Germany avoided the traumas which other Bloc countries underwent at a later stage.

Hungary had suffered a much more serious upheaval than any other country in the Bloc. Both the extensive purges and the revolution which followed them were indicative of the corruption and dissent within the ruling élite. The twists and turns of the government's policy between March 1956 and the outbreak of the revolution in the autumn demonstrated Rakosi's uncertainty about which course of action to follow. It was probably this hesitation which finally led to the breakdown of order and the uprising. But Rakosi was not the only Hungarian leader to hesitate. Imre Nagy also displayed hesitation about taking power and was 'in retirement, avoiding all political activity. Like Gomulka, only more passively, he was waiting for the party to summon him.' Nagy had earlier been accused of right-wing deviationism, and this, as well as personal prudence, may have played a part in his hesitation. With the benefit of hindsight it seems possible that, had he and other like-minded politicians displayed more determination during that fateful summer of 1956, the Hungarian process of change might have passed peacefully and the revolution would not have occurred. Eventually, after the Soviet intervention, the leadership was entrusted to Janos Kadar. This choice was an act of faith on the part of the Soviet leadership, because Kadar had supported the revolution as late as 1 November 1956; it was only on 4 November that he announced his break with Nagy on the radio and stated that he was forming a revolutionary workers' and peasants' government; a clear euphemism for a pro-Soviet leadership.

Nevertheless, in the context of the events which followed, Kadar appeared equally indecisive. There may have been good reasons for this, because one commentator noted that 'Kadar, like Nagy, dreamed at first of reconciling devotion to the party and loyalty to the USSR with patriotism, and even with Hungarian nationalism, of whose strength he was well aware.' However, when he found he had to make a choice between the two, he came down on the Soviet side. Whatever the reasons, hesitation seems to have played a large part in Kadar's actions – a hesitation difficult to understand, unless he, like Nagy, was waiting to see whether there would be any Western intervention in Hungary. There is, of course, also the possibility that Kadar, like other leaders who survived Stalinist purges, was simply too timid to take any chances. All these Communists, even the underground leader, Gomulka, seem to have displayed a greater measure of caution than of courage. The Stalinist period had left its mark on all the party leaders in the Bloc and it would take a great deal of protest from the population, or a great deal of its support, to force any of them to depart from the established policy. Even their apparent 'liberal' leanings were suspect. After the revolution was quelled, Kadar instituted a reign of terror which equalled that of Rakosi's; the political police were reconstituted and new, repressive, workers' militias were set up. These units were composed of the hardest Rakosi elements. 'Thus the Hungarians were given a new lesson in the terror they had freed themselves from in October. Excitement gave way to resignation, romantic nationalism to bitterly disillusioned realism.'

The Hungarian case showed that the new leaders were imbued with the same principles and spirit which had created Stalin and his entourage; and, indeed, little else could have been expected from this school of government. Though Stalin was dead and his ghost was being expurgated by Khrushchev, his legacy lived on, even if in a slightly diluted version. Only in one country, Poland, it appeared that a new spirit had entered the leadership. Boleslaw Bierut, an arch-Stalinist, was taken ill while in Moscow and died soon after the Twentieth Congress of the CPSU. On 20 March 1956, Edward Ochab was chosen as his successor. Ochab's main field of action had been the organisation of the party. However, he did not remain in power for long; in October 1956, eighteen months after his release from prison, Wladyslaw Gomulka was elected First Secretarty (though prolonged negotiations with Moscow delayed his confirmation for some time). Gomulka's first action was to introduce the changes which had long been demanded. However, Gomulka's rise to power was only made possible by a show of national solidarity which convinced the Soviet leadership that the Poles were determined to achieve a change. Gomulka himself raised various demands before he agreed to take power. It has been suggested that without this show of national solidarity, the Soviet authorities would not have conceded, but they 'seemed to have lost their heads at the prospect of a mounting wave of nationalism that might lead to the secession of Poland. . .'.[7]

Although Gomulka came to power on a strong wave of nationalist and anti-Soviet enthusiasm, he soon displayed his Stalinist credentials. When the Hungarian revolution occurred, he sided with the Soviet party in insisting that it be quelled. He did so despite violent Polish opposition to the Soviet intervention in Hungary, well aware that he was going against the wishes of even his own party. Once again, it was demonstrated that the new leaders were loyal to the CPSU in the first place, and that they would not deviate from this line in the face of protest from their own party or nation.

The Romanian attitude was somewhat different from that of the other countries in the Bloc. The Romanian leader, Gheorghiu Dej, was not opposed to a measure of nationalist feeling in the country, provided that this helped him to retain power. Because of this, his attitude towards the Hungarian uprising was more conciliatory than that of the other leaders. He even began to pay homage to the nationalist forces in Romania, a phenomenon which had been condemned since the end of the war. But such an attitude did not spell out any relaxation of police power, or any liberalisation. His successor has pursued similar policies, with the result that in the late 1980s Romania is the most Stalinist country in the Eastern Bloc, though it is the most anti-Soviet one.

Sufficient has been said above to demonstrate that every East European leader who was in power in 1956 was a Stalinist, though sometimes a covert one. Each one was ready and willing to use Stalinist tactics if threatened. The legacy Stalin had left was still very much alive, many years after his death, in the shape of the men in charge of government in the East European countries. It was as though Stalin's ghost was hovering over the region, unable to leave it, for fear of a relapse. Yet reforms were long overdue and new, far-thinking leadership was essential for Eastern Europe's future. The region had declined so much during the Stalinist period that only swift and decisive measures could remedy the situation.

Notes

1. For the former view, see Robert Conquest, *The Great Terror*; for the latter, Isaac Deutscher, *Stalin: A political biography*, particularly Chapter 9.
2. Deutscher, *Stalin*, pp. 378–80.
3. F. Claudin, *The Communist Movement: From Comintern to Cominform*, pp. 528–9.
4. F. Fejto, *A History of the People's Democracies: Eastern Europe since Stalin*, pp. 34–7 and 42–7.
5. Fejto, *A History*, pp. 142–3. Khrushchev made the speech in Sofia in June 1958, after withdrawing a large loan to Yugoslavia.
6. See Olga A. Narkiewicz, *Eastern Europe 1968–86*, Chapter 2, for the economic position in that period.
7. Information on pp. 22–6 has been culled from Fejto, *A History*, pp. 47–123.

2

Zhivkov: The grandfather of Communist Bulgaria

The antecedents of the Bulgarian Communist Party

Bulgaria, a small country in the Balkans, is often disregarded by political analysts. There is good reason for this, for though Bulgaria's history is ancient, its role in the last few centuries has been confined mainly to the Balkans. Its fate during the Second World War was governed by chance and mismanagement. The chance, which played an important part in Bulgaria's history, occurred when Hitler wanted to attack the USSR. In order to stop British interference, Hitler wanted to assure himself of secure control of the Balkans. Romania was already secured, but Greece had to be neutralised. This appeared to be relatively easy, as Bulgaria was prepared to help.

> On March 1st the Bulgarian Government swallowed his bribe and committed itself to a pact whereby the German forces were allowed to move through its territory and take up positions on the Greek frontier. The Soviet Government broadcast its disapproval of this departure from neutrality, but its abstention from anything more forcible made Hitler more sure that Russia was not ready for war.[1]

It has been often said, and with some truth, that the generals always fight the last war. The plan to occupy part of Greece was based on the German generals' recollections of the British landing in Salonika in 1915. It was therefore resolved that before an attack in the East would start, the Twelfth German Army would occupy the coast of Southern Thrace between Salonika and Dedeagach: 'The army assembled in Rumania, crossed the Danube into Bulgaria and from there was to pierce the Metaxas Line. . . .' Once the German forces reached the coast, the Bulgarian troops were to take over its protection, allowing the Germans to remove their troops. When presented with this plan, the King of Bulgaria, Tsar Boris, was doubtful, and expressed the fear that the Yugoslavs might threaten the flank of the army. However, he was assured that, in view of the pact between Nazi Germany and Yugoslavia, there was no danger of this. When German representatives tried to persuade him of this, 'They had the impression that King Boris was not quite convinced. He was proved right.' Just as the Twelfth Army was to begin its operations in Bulgaria, the Yugoslavs mounted a *coup* against the pro-Nazi regent, and the whole calculation unravelled. This, in turn, delayed the operation against the Soviet Union, postponing it from May till June and placed Bulgaria in the Nazi camp.[2]

Mismanagement followed chance. At the end of the war Bulgaria was in a farcical situation. Romania had capitulated to the Russians as soon as Soviet troops began to occupy her territory. Romania's capitulation spurred the Bulgarians to sue for peace, but not, paradoxically, with the advancing Soviet Union, but with Britain and the United States:

> For although it had abstained from joining the invasion of Russia, it had reason to be uneasy about the Russians' view of its neutrality. That fear was well justified. Bulgaria's readiness to submit to the Western Allies did not satisfy the Soviet government, which promptly declared war on Bulgaria, and followed this up with an immediate invasion from the east and north.

The invasion was simply a show of strength, because the Bulgarian government offered no resistance and promptly declared war on Nazi Germany.[3]

This account of Bulgaria's war adventures would probably qualify as a plot in a Ruritanian operetta, were it not for the serious consequences it had for the country and for the Balkans as a whole. Throughout the war period, the small and weak Communist Party of Bulgaria was illegal, as it had been before the war. Because of persecution, many Communists had been forced to live abroad for a long time, including the party leader, Dimitrov.

However, a small resistance movement was built up during the war; one of its most outstanding partisans was Traicho Kostov. By 1942, the Communists had established local committees of a 'Patriotic Front', and by 1943 a Central Committee of the Patriotic Front was set up. The committee included non-Communists and middle-class representatives. The Communists also formed a People's Liberation Army in 1943, and when the Red Army crossed into Bulgaria, the Liberation Army overthrew the old Bulgarian government on 9 September 1944. The new government of the Patriotic Front included Communists, peasant parties, social democrats and radical middle-class parties. The new government nationalised industries and collectivised agriculture in the face of strong national opposition.

Because of the opposition led by the peasant and social democratic parties, the Communist leader, Georgi Dimitrov, held a plebiscite on contentious issues. Eighty-eight per cent of the population voted, and of these, 86 per cent supported the Patriotic Front government. The newly established People's Assembly contained 94 Communists, 94 representatives of the Peasants' League, 31 social democrats and 56 middle class representatives. The new government continued its programme of collectivisation and nationalisation. In September 1946, 92.7 per cent of the Bulgarian electorate voted for the abolition of the monarchy; in October of the same year new elections were held for a Constituent Assembly. Nearly 70 per cent of the electorate voted for the Patriotic Front, a reduced majority compared with previous elections. By April 1947 all opposition parties were outlawed by the People's Court on the grounds that they were carrying out policies hostile to the Bulgarian people.[4]

This apparently effortless passage towards Communism belied the actual state of affairs. Bulgaria was an agricultural country, as the large number of peasant parties' representatives in the last free elections demonstrated. Collectivisation was opposed bitterly and led to the outlawing of peasant parties. The Bulgarian farmers never regained their influence in the country and, unlike the Polish farmers, never managed to reverse the collectivisation. While it may be argued that the Bulgarian economy actually profited by the collectivisation, the rift between the majority of the people and the goverment increased.

The Communist Party ruled, but it did not command a great

deal of respect. Two of its main leaders, Dimitrov and Kolarov, returned from Moscow after a long period in exile. They were elderly and spent: 'Dimitrov was already sixty-three when he returned to Bulgaria in 1945, a tired, ravaged hero. Kolarov was sixty-eight, and in very poor health.'[5] Dimitrov had enjoyed tremendous prestige in the Soviet Union, having been the hero of the Reichstag fire trial; his name was 'the symbol of militant antifascism. Stalin demonstrated his personal association with Dimitrov on every possible occasion – the Bulgarian leader invariably appeared at his side at ceremonies and parades.'[6]

Dimitrov's past history is of some interest. He became the head of the Comintern at the Seventh Congress in 1935, and was instrumental in creating the policy of European popular fronts. By the mid-1940s he may have become too liberal for Stalin's liking, possibly because of his broad international experience. After the liberation of Bulgaria (as the Communists called it), he expressed hopes that a new Bulgarian socialist state could be constructed as a result of co-operation between the working classes and the peasants, with the close involvement of the middle classes and the intellectuals. However, the beginning of the Cold War forced him to take the hard line enforced by Stalin. When the opposition parties were outlawed in 1947, Dimitrov announced that the dictatorship of the proletariat continued to be as necessary in the 1940s as it had been in the 1920s, and that a 'people's democracy' fulfilled the functions of such a dictatorship.[7]

Despite such pronouncements, Dimitrov showed a great degree of independence when he discussed the idea of a Balkan federation with Tito as early as 1944. When, at the request of Stalin, the talks were interrupted, the two leaders resumed them in 1947. Meeting at a conference in Bled, Yugoslavia, they produced a series of agreements which would have resulted in a federation. The federation never came into being, for reasons which are very complicated. However, in January 1948, Dimitrov outlined an even bigger project: the creation of a Balkan and Danubian federation, which would have included all the People's Democracies, as well as Greece. Strangely enough, in view of his supposed expansionist policies, Stalin was strongly opposed to the idea. By the end of January *Pravda* published a statement opposing the project; in February Stalin summoned Dimitrov and Kardelj to Moscow and scolded them severely. He went so far as to tell Dimitrov that he was acting as though he was still the Secretary of the Comintern. It has been commented that the idea of a federation 'was undoubtedly connected with the idea that it was necessary to follow new roads, different from the Soviet one, in the march towards socialism. . . . Its principal theoretician – in so far as one can talk of theoretical development here – was Dimitrov himself.'[8]

It has since become well known that the project of the Balkan federation was one of the main points of conflict between Tito and Stalin, but it is doubtful whether Dimitrov was the father of 'Eurocommunism', or of a 'separate road to socialism', as one writer maintains. Rather, one must regard Dimitrov as an old man at the end of his days, looking for ways of strengthening his country and avoiding future wars. The project was subject to Stalin's approval. When Stalin vetoed it, Dimitrov abandoned the idea and left Tito to face the Soviet Union on his own.

Dimitrov was a sick man at this stage. He went for treatment to Moscow in January 1949 and died there in July of the same year. Kolarov died soon after Dimitrov, in January 1950. The old generation of Communist fighters had passed away, and the field was open for successors. The natural successor would have been Kostov, but there were other home-based Communists who had a strong claim to succession. Kostov was not acceptable to Stalin because of his independent attitudes, particularly after the split with Yugoslavia. A new, 'Muscovite' leader had to be found; he soon emerged in the person of Vulko Chervenkov – an unexpected choice.

> 'What is important to note here, however, is that in the early postwar period very few people imagined he would achieve power. He had been in the Soviet Union since 1925 but had not been prominent among the Bulgarian exiles there and was little known in Bulgaria itself. . . . He returned to Bulgaria only in 1946 to become the Chairman of the Committee on Science, Art and Culture, a post that hardly seemed the stepping stone to supreme political power. But he had three things on his side: first, he did have brains, personality and ruthlessness; second, he had married Georgi Dimitrov's sister; third . . . he was trusted by the Soviets. . . .'[9]

In 1950 Chervenkov became the prime minister and first secretary of the party. He quickly removed all the home-based Communists from their posts, replacing them with 'Muscovites', or younger, home-based functionaries. Among the latter was Todor Zhivkov. Chervenkov then began to Sovietise Bulgaria, modelling his government on the Stalinist pattern. That may have appeared rather strange in view of Chervenkov's personal history, which was quite unusual in the context of Bulgarian Communism. He was born in 1900, the son of a non-commissioned officer and graduated from a Sofia *gymnasium*. He was active against Bulgaria's participation in the First World War, and joined the Communist Party in 1919. After it was found that he had been involved in a bomb plot against King Boris in 1925, he had to go into exile. On arrival in Moscow, he attended the Marx-Engels Institute and, after graduating, lectured there. In view of his long stay in the Soviet Union and his involvement with theory, there was no doubt that he was ideologically sound and personally loyal to Stalin and the CPSU.[10]

Though Chervenkov suffered a personal setback when Stalin died soon after his own accession to power, he soon adapted to the new situation. The police terror was relaxed; it became easier to travel abroad; even some emigration was allowed. Chervenkov himself set a good example and became more accessible to the public. However, the biggest changes were made at the top of the party. Chervenkov placed Todor Zhivkov in the post of first secretary, while he himself retained the post of prime minister. This was probably Chervenkov's biggest mistake, for Zhivkov, then forty-two years old, soon became a serious rival for power.

Zhivkov was born in 1911 in a poor, peasant family and had had little formal education. He studied at the High School of Drawing and Engraving in Sofia and became a printer by trade. He joined the underground Young Communist League in 1928; in due course he became a party member and a member of the Sofia District Party Committee. During the Second World War he established a good record in the resistance movement and became a full member of the Party Central Committee at the Fifth Congress in 1948. From then on, he rose rapidly in the Sofia organisation and by 1950 had become a secretary of the Central Committee and a candidate member of the Politburo, becoming a full member in 1951.[11]

Despite his rapid ascent, Zhivkov had not been considered a candidate for supreme power. It had been suggested that the most serious candidate was Georgi Chankov (Tsankov), but that Chervenkov chose Zhivkov rather than Chankov, because the latter was too intelligent. In fact, Zhivkov played a very minor role in the government for the first two years in office. But by 1956, when he became a protégé of Khrushchev, Zhivkov forced Chervenkov to step down somewhat and assume the lower post of first deputy prime minister. By then Zhivkov also felt sufficiently secure to rehabilitate the purged leaders. On 11 April 1956 he announced at a meeting of Sofia activists that the charges against Kostov and his associates had been false. While it was too late for Kostov, who had been hanged in December 1949, the survivors of the trial were released from prison, rehabilitated and readmitted to the party.[12]

In the following period Zhivkov performed many difficult and dangerous manoeuvres, the outcome of which turned out badly for Chervenkov. Several versions of the infighting exist,[13] but the outcome was inevitable: Zhivkov, the younger man, won. In May 1962 Khrushchev visited Sofia to strengthen Zhivkov's authority and calm Bulgaria's fears about the recent Soviet reconciliation with Yugoslavia.[14] Khrushchev's visit helped to establish Zhivkov's ascendancy over his rivals, Anton Yugov, Georgi Chankov and Vulko Chervenkov, at the next party congress in November 1962. After the congress, Zhivkov became the prime minister, as well as retaining his post as first secretary. He now felt secure enough to begin cautious moves towards reforms. He also proceeded to shift his loyalties towards the CPSU. 'Zhivkov . . . lost little time in switching his allegiance to the new CPSU leadership of Brezhnev and Kosygin, which replaced Khrushchev in 1964. This transfer of loyalty obviously suggests that for Zhivkov the support of CPSU leadership is a necessity which transcends loyalty to any one Soviet party leader,' commented one analyst. However, he contended that 'while Zhivkov has managed to remain in power by courting the Soviet Union and outmanœuvring political rivals, he has never really succeeded in establishing a relationship of legitimate "authority" either within the party or among the population.' Zhivkov was classified as an *apparatchik*, a man who rose through the party ranks, whose claim to the status of a leader was artificial and unconvincing.[15]

Though this analysis may have been correct, Zhivkov certainly seized the reins of power after 1961. 'After his triumph at the Eighth Party Congress in 1962, Zhivkov had no serious rival in the top echelons of the Bulgarian Communist Party.' Following his appointment as first secretary, he managed to remove Chervenkov, Chankov and Yugov from the political scene, though all these men had been much more powerful than he in the former days. However, Zhivkov's triumph nearly came to a very bad end in 1965. The origins of the alleged anti-Zhivkov plot are obscure. But it is certain that the outcome was dramatic and destroyed a number of senior party members and military officers.

The story which has emerged is as follows. On the night of 7 April 1965, Ivan Todorov-Gorunya, a senior party member, shot himself in his Sofia apartment to avoid arrest by the security police. This was a new phenomenon in Communist Bulgaria. Plots had been rife in Bulgaria up to the Second World War, but this appeared to have been the first one in the Communist period. 'The full story of what happened probably will never be known in the West,' commented one writer. But in a speech to senior army officers, broadcast by Radio Sofia on 8 May of that year, Zhivkov stated that there had been a group of plotters which, he claimed, consisted of no more than five alienated people. The plot seems to have been engineered by a group of ex-partisans, by then all senior military officers and party members, but with strong roots in regional party organisations. But further evidence contradicts Zhivkov's statement. There must have been more than five conspirators, because at the trial there were nine defendants, not counting the dead leader. 'The partisan movement in Bulgaria was never very strong. . . . It had little popular support and fought not so much against the Germans . . . but against Bulgarian army and police units sent to hunt them down.' When the war ended, the partisans expected to be rewarded, and it is certain that they were disappointed with the posts which they had been allotted, having expected more senior positions. However, the most senior posts went to the 'Muscovites' and the partisans felt that they had been denied the fruits of their victory. Even more damaging was the fact that some of them were physically persecuted.[16]

Under the circumstances, it is not surprising that they took to plotting. However, (probably thanks to Zhivkov's superior spies) the conspiracy was uncovered and the conspirators sentenced to various terms of imprisonment; Zhivkov himself survived. But the structure of the plot and its timing are interesting. The plot occurred a few months after the removal of Khrushchev from office in October 1964. Zhivkov had been Khrushchev's protégé. Was the plot an attempt by Khrushchev's successors to remove his friends from office? Or was it, as some sources suggest, an attempt by the military to move Bulgaria out of the Soviet orbit and into a pro-Chinese orbit?[17] One will probably have to wait for some time yet for Zhivkov's successor to reveal the real reason for the plot – always assuming that there was a plot. However, if the story has some basis in fact, then it demonstrates that military plots and assassination attempts are far more common within the Bloc than is generally assumed. The perfect order, discipline and monolithic nature of the party, as perceived from the outside, are but an illusion. While power struggles are no doubt often exaggerated, it is probably true that hostility erupts periodically in a violent form – usually planned and executed by the military.

The successful eradication of the plotters strengthened Zhivkov's position, particularly after he removed another rival, Mitko Grigorov, from the Politburo in 1966. By 1971 he had been in power long enough to be criticised for being autocratic. Protests were voiced about the decision-making process and a Central Committee Plenum adopted a resolution in October of that year, stating that the Central Committee should be informed about the work of the Politburo and the Secretariat. However, by then, Zhivkov was thoroughly ensconced in office and, with the departure of Ulbricht in East Germany, he was the longest ruling first secretary in the Bloc. Though he was to enjoy yet greater triumphs in the years to come, it may be that the very length of his stay in office told against him in the end.

There were also other problems. Criticisms of Zhivkov's style of government may have been due to the party's annoyance at his subservience to Moscow. Such subservience was then becoming unfashionable in the Bloc and the new generation of Communists resented it. In addition, the younger officials were getting impatient for more power. But Zhivkov's political skills stood him in good stead: 'Reliant on Moscow to buttress his domestic power, Zhivkov has been among the most loyal and obedient of the Soviet Union's Warsaw Pact allies in matters of foreign policy.' And since the Soviet Union would find it very difficult to select another leader as loyal as Zhivkov, his chances of staying in office for much longer were very good.[18]

It turned out, however, that Zhivkov's concentration on good relations with Moscow was only part of a much broader plan, a plan which he unfolded over the later years of his leadership. On the internal front, his government carried out significant economic reforms, which altered the former agricultural country almost completely. Externally, he set about developing relations with both socialist and capitalist countries, which was to prove useful for Bulgaria's development. The extent of his success was not fully apparent till the late 1970s and early 1980s. But even in the late 1960s it was clear that the reforms were bearing some fruit.

An observer may be interested to enquire how Zhivkov, a man who started from very humble beginnings, had little formal education, and spent most of his earlier life in party service, came to play such a dominant, and later on, positive, role in his country and in the Bloc. Many analysts have suggested that he had a talent for self-effacement, even as he continued to climb up the ladder of promotion. Nevertheless, he gained the highest office in his country, and then had to use all his skills to retain it. Zhivkov has few earmarks of a tyrant, but the impression he has given is not that of a gentle personality. During his climb to supreme power he managed to wipe out all domestic opposition, and it has been demonstrated that he did not do so through the power of persuasion. He also managed to obtain – or retain – the trust of all the successive Soviet leaders. He personally maintained control of both domestic and foreign policies, and developed a new line in both of them. He pursued a slow, but steady, policy of development, managing to do so without much political liberalisation. And finally he made Bulgaria, the most underdeveloped country in the Bloc, into one of the most technologically successful ones – all this without any previous technological or industrial base to build upon.

As he continued in power, Zhivkov's personality began to take on a new hue. No longer the obedient *apparatchik* (though he always maintained cordial relations with the Soviet Union and supported most Soviet foreign policies), Zhivkov grew in stature on the international scene. He always manged to appear conciliatory and reasonable at international conferences, and often acted as the spokesman for the Bloc. Much of his mild manner was probably due to his neutral looks. His photographs from the late 1960s and early 1970s show a balding, well-groomed, middle-aged man, whose only distinction were his deep-set eyes. His appearance was so bland that unless one knew him, one would find it difficult to realise that he was a virtual dictator in his own country. But there was more substance to Zhivkov than a bland appearance and an apparently bland set of policies.

This became apparent in the early 1980s, when the new Soviet leadership began its insistent demands for changes in the system of government in the Bloc. Zhivkov almost immediately grasped the issues involved, and showed himself to be supple, adaptable and responsive to the changed situation. Though already an old man, he demonstrated that his mind was by no means petrified and that he was ready to meet the Soviet challenge half-way. A student of the history of the Church, particularly the Byzantine one, might see in Zhivkov some similarity with clerical dignitaries in ancient times. Ruthless when necessary, benevolent when things go well, Zhivkov had all the manipulative skills of a successful prince of the Church. Though he lacks charisma, he always gives the impression of being in charge, and of coping with his task. One could well imagine that he is a throw-back to the old traditions of Slavonic Christianity that gave Bulgaria its prestige centuries earlier – though, of course, Zhivkov's religion is not Christianity but Communism, and he is its major and most senior priest in his country.

Zhivkov's foreign policy

Perhaps nowhere is Zhivkov's skill seen more vividly than in his patient and consistent attempts to develop Bulgaria's foreign policy in the face of manifold difficulties. Bulgaria had little or no political standing in Europe before the Second World War. It did not have a powerful army like Poland; it had no natural resources like Romania; its borders did not have the same strategic importance as those of Czechoslovakia – as a result its government did not carry much weight in international relations. While Bulgaria was relatively isolated in the Balkans, its main foreign orientation was directed at Germany; and perhaps because of this, Germany was its chief economic partner in the inter-war period.

It says a lot for Zhivkov's realism that, instead of bearing a grudge to Germany for bringing Bulgaria into a disastrous war, he began to build on the traditions of past co-operation. In the early 1960s, the Bulgarians badly needed advanced technology, which was at this stage only available from the Federal Republic. Bonn was ready to open up the Bulgarian market again, and Zhivkov exchanged trade missions with the Federal Republic in March 1964, signing a bilateral trade treaty for a two-year period. After the removal of Khrushchev in 1964, the Soviet leadership crisis allowed Zhivkov to improve relations with Germany. This was soon demonstrated by the 'Peace Note' episode. In March 1966 the West German government sent a memorandum to all the countries in the Socialist Bloc, urging them to improve their relations with Germany. All the East European countries replied negatively, with the exception of Bulgaria and Romania, which did not reply, or did not make their replies public. However, Bonn's appeal to Eastern Europe was seen by Moscow as dangerous, particularly after Romania established formal diplomatic relations with the Federal Republic on 31 January 1967. Always mindful of his first loyalties, Zhivkov launched an attack on the West German *Ostpolitik* at the next Warsaw Pact meeting in April 1967. As a result of this attack, relations between West Germany and Bulgaria remained frozen for the rest of the 1960s, and did not become cordial again till the beginning of the *détente*.[19]

The two countries' relations were eventually mended when Zhivkov visited the Federal Republic on an official visit in November 1975. This event was hailed as a great breakthrough in diplomacy. By that time Zhivkov was head of state as well as first secretary and his host was the West German president, Walter Scheel. It was the first time that a Bulgarian head of state had visited West Germany since the end of the Second World War, and the visit was a long one; it lasted five days, from 24 to 28 November. The size of the delegation alone spoke for the importance which was attached to the visit. The Bulgarian group numbered fifty people and included the first deputy prime minister, Petar Tanchev; the foreign minister, Petar Mladenov; deputy prime minister, Ognyan Doynov (who was in charge of co-operation with capitalist countries), as well as several other top officials. In keeping with tradition, the delegation also included Zhivkov's 22-year-old son, Vladimir.

The visit was in return for President Scheel's official visit to Bulgaria as foreign minister in March 1974, soon after the re-establishment of West German–Bulgarian relations in December 1973. The West German media reported Zhivkov's visit at length. A number of newspapers provided a political portrait, biographical data and assessed his foreign policy.[20] The coverage in the Bulgarian press was also ample, though this was traditional when Zhivkov visited abroad. An editorial in *Rabotnichesko Delo* on 24

November even praised the Federal Republic's *Ostpolitik*, claiming that the Bulgarian nation had a high regard for the political realism of the current West German government.

The Germans had good reason to get excited about Zhivkov's visit. In 1974 Bulgaria's imports of West German goods increased by 84 per cent, while Bulgarian exports to Germany declined. Bulgaria's trade deficit with the Federal Republic amounted to 530 million Deutschmarks in 1974, and was expected to reach 700 million Deutschmarks in 1975.[21] In an interview broadcast over the German television networks on 23 November, Zhivkov emphasised the necessity of overcoming the political and trade-exchange difficulties and of developing a pattern of balanced trade relations. Playing the role of an elder statesman, he talked about *détente*, criticising 'certain Western circles which have launched a campaign in the information media . . . aimed at hindering the process of *détente* and intended to arouse suspicion of the peaceful policy of the socialist countries'. He also spoke in favour of co-operation in Europe among countries with different socio-political systems, instead of focusing on ideological differences: 'That is why we oppose those circles, which are attempting to make use of the ideological differences in a cold-war spirit,' he said and reminded the audience that Bulgaria and the Federal Republic had now established a realistic system of co-operation, despite their political differences.[22]

Zhivkov did not neglect other means of communicating his views. During his two days of talks in Bonn, he met Willy Brandt, Helmut Kohl and a number of leading West German businessmen. On 25 November he opened the new Bulgarian Embassy and received the chairman of the West German Communist Party, Herbert Mies, with whom he discussed the international Communist movement. Also on 25 November he met Chancellor Schmidt, with whom he had already made acquaintance at the Helsinki Conference. The two leaders discussed bilateral economic relations and current political problems. At the end of the meeting, which lasted an hour and a half, three agreements were signed. These dealt with economic, scientific and technological co-operation and with cultural exchanges; they also contained a statement on the need to improve relations between the two nations in accordance with UNO statutes and the Helsinki Accords. It was stated that such an improvement was necessary in order to strengthen world peace and promote international *détente*.

These objectives are not really startling, for they were identical with the objectives of the Brezhnev leadership which had been promoting them for some time. It would appear, therefore, that Zhivkov had been chosen as the spokesman for the Soviet Union and the rest of the Bloc to discuss matters of utmost importance and urgency for the Soviet leadership of that period. It is clear that the Soviet government had the utmost confidence in Zhivkov, to entrust him with such a crucial task. Otherwise, he would have been unable to make the kind of statements he did at this sensitive juncture in East–West relations; the expression of such views would almost certainly have had to have been sanctioned by Moscow.

It can be seen, therefore, that in a relatively short period of time, Zhivkov was transformed from a provincial *apparatchik* (for Bulgaria was a provincial country) into a spokesperson for the Soviet Union's and the Warsaw Pact's most vital interests. To a certain extent, this may have been a legacy due to the influence of the deceased Dimitrov, the spokesman for the Comintern; but there were additional reasons for the choice. First, Zhivkov was obviously willing to follow Soviet dictates, as the volte-face on relations with West Germany demonstrated; second, he must have been considered a good diplomat; and third, as leader of a relatively unimportant country, he could be entrusted with tasks the Soviet leadership did not want to undertake itself. If the initiatives misfired, the blame would be Zhivkov's, not the Soviet Union's. The fact that most of Zhivkov's missions can be deemed to have been successful underlines the extent of Soviet indebtedness to his efforts. And that may have been the reason that he retained his post for much longer than any other East European leader.

Other factors may also have played a role. Zhivkov happened to be acceptable to both the East and the West. While Romanians were (at this stage) acceptable to the West, they were not popular with the Soviet leadership. The East Germans were only just beginning to emerge from the seclusion which they had imposed on themselves at the end of the 1960s; the Czechoslovaks were shunned by the West for a long period after the events of 1968; and the Poles and the Hungarians were considered to be unreliable by the Soviet Union. In this schema, the emergence of a Bulgarian leader – perhaps without the qualities of Dimitrov, but not an unfit successor to him – must have suited the Soviet Union very well. Zhivkov was sufficiently self-effacing not to be feared, diplomatic enough to be confided in, and loyal enough to be trusted. Zhivkov, in fact, fulfilled the role of a faithful emissary very well and, as will be seen later, he performed it perfectly.

The visit to West Germany was the culmination of a very busy year for Zhivkov. He had already made several important visits in that year; he had contributed to the Helsinki Conference, and had visited Italy and Algeria. As in the case of West Germany, the Italian visit was the first to be paid by a Bulgarian head of state since the end of the Second World War; hence, it had an added significance. For this visit, Zhivkov was accompanied by his daughter, Lyudmilla (who, since the death of his wife, had generally acted as Bulgaria's first lady on his official trips to non-Communist countries); by the foreign minister, Petar Mladenov; the foreign trade minister, Ivan Nedenev, and other senior officials. A communiqué issued at the end of the official part of his visit described the talks with President Giovanni Leone and Prime Minister Aldo Moro (who was later murdered by a terrorist group) as friendly and constructive.[23]

On the last day of his stay, 27 June, Zhivkov was received by Pope Paul vi in a forty-minute private audience. The Vatican visit was another 'first' for Zhivkov, who addressed the pontiff in French. According to a Vatican spokesman, his speech was characterised by 'cordiality and courtesy'. Bulgaria and the Vatican had never had diplomatic relations and this, according to the commentators, explained why a private audience was granted. However, it seems more likely that the Vatican was keen to give special treatment to a leader of a Communist country, whose main religion was Orthodox. The Catholic Church had for a long time hoped for a union with the Eastern Churches. The visit of a Communist leader, whose country who had been the pioneer of Slavonic Christianity (and who, despite his professions of atheism, was deeply aware of this tradition) was an appropriate moment to bring this union one step nearer. Hence, if Zhivkov acted as an ambassador of peace for the Soviet leadership, he may have appeared to the Vatican as the bearer of a new message from the Socialist Bloc: that of a reconciliation not only between the East and the West, but also between Eastern and Western rites.

Indeed, when the final communiqué was issued after the audience, it was noted that the situation of the Catholic Church, 'both the Latin and the Byzantine–Slavic rites', in Bulgaria had been discussed, and the Pope was reported to have expressed the hope 'that Catholics would continue to be permitted religious freedom in Bulgaria, which is in any case guaranteed by [its] Constitution.' The pontiff was clearly as diplomatic as Zhivkov, for he could not have been ignorant of the fact that religious practice was strongly discouraged in Bulgaria, and that his visitor had not the slightest intention of relaxing the Communist regime and promoting religion, beyond maintaining the barest appearance of religious freedom.

However, though an atheist, Zhivkov had a strong belief in the historical mission of the Bulgarians, who had proselytised among the Slavs – a tradition of which he was proud. To underline his respect for this tradition, Zhivkov opened an exhibition of Bulgarian icons and visited the Basilica of St Clement, which houses the tomb of St Cyril, the 'Apostle of the Slavs'. During this visit, Lyudmilla Zhivkova expressed the Bulgarian people's gratitude for the care taken of St Cyril's tomb by the Vatican and the Italian government, while Zhivkov laid a wreath of flowers on the tomb. A mosaic panel and a silver wreath with an inscription bearing Todor Zhivkov's name were unveiled to celebrate the memory of the creators of the Slavonic alphabet, St Cyril and St Methodius.[24] This strange ceremony must surely have been the first time that a Communist leader has been honoured in this way by a major Church; and it probably marked another important occasion in Zhivkov's calendar.

Having travelled to so many countries with his message, Zhivkov then set down his thoughts in an article published at the end of 1976, entitled 'A Year of Peace, a Year of Struggle', which was specially written for the December 1976 issue of *Problems of Peace and Socialism*. The article was divided into four sections; the first section dealt with the problems of *détente*, the Helsinki Accords and the contribution of the Soviet Union and other socialist countries to these developments. The author praised Leonid Brezhnev's role in this process, using the occasion of his seventieth birthday. He then proceeded to sum up Bulgaria's economic achievements and to discuss the integration of the Comecon as well as the co-ordination of the foreign policy of the Bloc. The third section of the article was entitled *Internationalism and Détente*, and contained the essence of the argument. It began with the statement that during 1976 – an important year from the Eurocommunist point of view – the Bulgarian party had paid special attention to the principles of 'proletarian internationalism'.

To sum up briefly, Zhivkov argued that proletarian internationalism (a code name for anti-Eurocommunism) is not incompatible with *détente*, and that Bulgaria was in favour of *détente*. He further strengthened his arguments by references to the father of Bulgarian Communism and the head of the Comintern, Georgi Dimitrov. The latter was quoted as having said that 'fraternal solidarity with the Soviet Union is the touchstone of internalionalism'. This definition, Zhivkov maintained, was valid even in the current period, because the Soviet Union was the 'nucleus around which the socialist community crystallizes'. This quotation was used as a starting point for an attack on Eurocommunism which, it was said, had been invented by bourgeois propaganda and was intended to divide the socialist countries and parties. Eurocommunism, the argument went, would prove dangerous for the Bloc and the non-ruling Communist parties. Although the gist of the article was a sustained attack on Eurocommunism, there was no intention to burn the bridges completely, as some conciliatory phrases were included. However, these might simply have been sentiments which a skilled diplomat like Zhivkov could be expected to pronounce.[25]

Just as in 1975, during the heyday of *détente* and co-operation after the Helsinki Conference, Zhivkov had played the role of a spokesman for the Bloc, so at the end of 1976, which saw the ill-fated Berlin conference of Communist parties and the rapid growth of Eurocommunism, he spoke for the hardline elements in the Soviet Politburo (probably Suslov himself), and put his reputation on the line to defend the anti-Eurocommunist stand of some top members of the Politburo of the CPSU. However, he did so with some subtlety: the Bulgarian party had to maintain good relations with the Eurocommunist PCI (the Italian communist party), and did not wish to spoil the working relationship with other European parties which may have been inclined towards Eurocommunism. Nevertheless, in time of need, the hardliners in the CPSU knew they could count on Zhivkov; always mindful of his duty to the Soviet Union and his devotion to socialism (and probably worried about retaining office because of his advancing age), he would put Soviet requests for help above the needs of the Communist movement as a whole. In the final analysis, he was wise not to attack the Eurocommunists too violently, for a decade later, while he was still in office, the new Soviet leadership under Gorbachev almost institutionalised Eurocommunism and made *glasnost* a tenet of Soviet restructuring. However, by that time the original trend of Eurocommunism had also changed; it was no longer dramatically anti-Soviet, but rather much more pro-European and internationalist in character. In addition, the Eurocommunist concepts must have been readily understood by Zhivkov, a Bulgarian who had once hoped for a Balkan federation. A 'Europe from the Atlantic to the Urals' might be a welcome development for a small country and Zhivkov could well forget his previous criticisms and adhere to the new course. Such an action would not have been the first time Zhivkov changed his mind.

Zhivkov and the Bulgarian economic miracle

Zhivkov's record in developing Bulgarian science and technology is unmatched in the Socialist Bloc. He came to power when the country was a backward, agrarian society, and he set out to achieve a technological revolution. Judging by the results, he was very successful for two decades. Zhivkov announced the decision to introduce technological development at the July 1968 Plenum, when he stated that the intention was to 'direct special attention to Bulgarian science and the working out and implementation of the proper strategy and tactics in the sphere of science policy'.[26]

According to the project, automated systems were to serve a total of 70 per cent of the Bulgarian economy by 1975; in 1971 alone, the number of computers was to increase fivefold, and the funds for scientific research were to be increased by 15 per cent above the 1970 allocation. The number of scientific specialists was to double between the years 1971 and 1975.[27] Zhivkov's role in this ambitious project must not be overlooked. Though he himself was not responsible for the concept and the planning, he was far-sighted enough to see the importance of science and technology, to start the process of modernisation, and – most importantly – to devote ample funds for such developments.

In view of these progressive policies, the ridicule with which the average age of the Bulgarian Politburo was treated rings rather hollow. All or most of Bulgaria's ills were attributed to the elderly leadership. Noting the tensions among the Bulgarian intellectuals and working classes, one observer stated that these tensions were scarely recognised by the government.

> In order to effect the desired transformation, the BCP must have an imaginative and innovative leadership, but today Bulgaria has the dubious distinction of having the oldest Politburo in Eastern Europe. One member, the Stalinist relic Todor Pavlov, is over 80, and three – Boyan Balgaranov, Ivan Mikhailov and Tsola Dragoycheva – are in their mid-70's. Todor Zhivkov himself is 61. Moreover, the present ruling elite can look back on an average of almost 40 years of membership of the BCP: all the full members of the Politburo . . . entered the party before September 9, 1944, the day of Bulgaria's 'liberation' by Soviet troops. . . .[28]

Nearly two decades later, in 1988, the by then 77-year-old Zhivkov still refused to resign. Moreover, as one journalist put it, Moscow was getting bad signals from Sofia. Khudomir Alexandrov, one of the main 'renovators', and several of his colleagues were dismissed from their posts in the summer of 1988. Zhivkov was apparently annoyed that the reforms they advocated might upset the status quo. For the first time since his discussions with Tito, many decades earlier, Zhivkov opposed the Soviet leadership actively. This may be because he is too old to institute any changes, over and above those which he himself had begun; but it may also be because he considers himself as an 'elder statesman' of the Bloc, and thinks that Gorbachev is a mere youngster. An observer might think that Mr Gorbachev could learn a lot of useful things from an old 'survivor' like Zhivkov, particularly since, in his younger days, Zhivkov was a technocratic wizard of the kind to which Gorbachev aspires.[29]

However, it is certain that Zhivkov's days are numbered, if only because of his advancing years. Younger, better educated people are waiting impatiently to take over the reins of power. But it remains to be seen whether they will enjoy the same successes that Zhivkov has done. At the end of his period, Zhivkov appears almost like an ideal East European leader: ruthless when necessary, but benevolent when possible; a loyal ally who managed to unite progressive ideas with traditional values; a good diplomat and a good family man. If there is another, less bland and smooth personality under his mask, then one will have to wait for his retirement for it to emerge.

Notes

1. B.H. Liddell Hart, *History of the Second World War*, p. 158.
2. *Ibid.*, pp. 139–40.
3. *Ibid.*, pp. 612–13.
4. The above information is based on that given by Jürgen Tampke, *The People's Republics of Eastern Europe*, pp. 22–3.
5. J.F. Brown, *Bulgaria under Communist Rule*, p. 21.
6. Deutscher, *Stalin*, p. 420.
7. Claudin, *The Communist Movement*, pp. 461–2.
8. *Ibid.*, pp. 489–91.
9. Brown, *Bulgaria*, pp. 21–2. Strangely enough, Lyudmilla Zhivkova, Todor Zhivkov's daughter, has held an identical post.
10. Brown, *Bulgaria*, p.23.
11. B. Lewytzkyj and J. Stroynowski, *Who's Who in Socialist Countries*, and Brown, *Bulgaria*, p.32.
12. Fejto, *A History*, p. 86.
13. For instance, see the conflicting reports in Fejto, *A History*, and Brown, *Bulgaria*.
14. Fejto, *A History*, pp. 182–3.
15. F. Stephen Larrabee, 'Bulgaria's politics of conformity, *Problems of Communism*, July–August 1972.
16. Brown, *Bulgaria*, pp. 173–9.
17. Larrabee, 'Bulgaria's politics'.
18. *Ibid.*
19. *Ibid.*
20. *Die Welt*, 22, 24, 26 and 27 November 1975; *Frankfurter Rundschau*, 24 November 1975; *Handelsblatt*, 24 November 1975; *Die Zeit*, 27 November 1975.
21. RFE (Radio Free Europe), *Situation Report*, Munich, Bulgaria/33, 4 December 1975.
22. Television interview, as reported by RFE *Situation Report*, Bulgaria/33.
23. RFE, *Situation Report*, Bulgaria/19, 11 July 1975.
24. RFE, *Situation Report*, Bulgaria/19.
25. RFE, *Situation Report*, Bulgaria/31, 8 December 1976.
26. Zhivkov's speech at the Plenum, quoted by Larrabee, 'Bulgaria's politics'.

27. Bulgaria's economic progress has been discussed in Narkiewicz, *Eastern Europe*, Chapter 2, pp. 52–6 and Chapter 5, pp. 131–5.
28. Larrabee, 'Bulgaria's politics'.
29. 'La Bulgarie à reculons', *Le Monde*, 24–5 July 1988.

3

The changing leadership in Czechoslovakia

The origins of the Czechoslovak problems

All European Communist parties have had a varied and often difficult history, but some have suffered more turbulence than others. The history of the Czechoslovak Communist Party is perhaps one of the most interesting. This is due partly to the fact that after the Nazi take-over of power in Germany, and the Dolfuss *putsch* in Austria, Czechoslovakia was the only country in Central Europe which still had a legal Communist party. Moreover, the strength of that party was manifest, and its roots, particularly in the industrial Bohemia, were deep. In Slovakia, an agrarian and strongly Catholic region, the Communist Party's grip was smaller, but as the 1930s recession began to affect the farmers, the party grew gradually. The importance of the Communist Party was so well attested that even after the partition of Czechoslovakia at Munich, its deputies continued to sit in the post-Munich parliament. Its leader, Antonin Zapotocky, was even able to make a pro-Soviet speech from the floor of the Chamber of Deputies.[1]

When Czechoslovakia was completely dismembered by the Nazis in March 1939, many party leaders went into hiding; others were arrested by the Gestapo and sent to concentration camps. Zapotocky was one of the captured leaders. Some senior Communists, however, managed to escape abroad, and while several went to France and Britain, the majority of the top leadership,

Gottwald, Slansky and many others, went to Moscow, where they set up party headquarters in exile. After the conclusion of the Soviet–German Non-aggression Pact in August 1939, the Czech Communists became an embarrassment to Stalin, eager, at that time, to appease Hitler. Their position improved somewhat after the German invasion of the Soviet Union, but even then Stalin found them superfluous. He began to court the Czechoslovak government – headed by President Benes – in exile in London. There are accounts to the effect that, during Benes' first official visit to Moscow in December 1943, neither Stalin nor the foreign minister, Molotov, mentioned the Communist leaders once. When the Gottwald group was invited to the ceremonies given for the Czech delegation, it was accorded scant attention, while all the honours were directed at the Benes party.

It was only towards the end of 1944 that Gottwald and his colleagues began to be groomed for government. By January 1945 the process was so well advanced that, in a letter to President Benes about the future of Ruthenia (then still part of pre-partition Czechoslovakia), Stalin specifically mentioned that he had discussed the matter with Comrade Gottwald.[2] After the Red Army entered Czechoslovakia, crucial negotiations were held in Moscow in March 1945. The formation of a new Czechoslovak government was being discussed and the discussions were dominated by Gottwald and his colleagues. The non-Communist delegates who arrived from London were presented with a copy of a new 'Programme for the government of the National Front of Czechs and Slovaks', which they accepted, though with some hesitation. The Communists also drew up a list of ministerial posts which they wanted to hold, including the key positions of ministers of the interior, defence, information and education, which were to be reserved for them. Other key posts were also assigned to the Communists or their close allies.

Analysing the changed situation, one historian asked:

> How did they attain such spectacular success? The answer lies not only in the situation prevailing at that time in Czechoslovakia but also in the relations between Soviet Russia and the Western Powers. The Red Army was deep in Czechoslovakia. . . . The same process was evident throughout the rest of Eastern Europe. . . . It thus became obvious that the Soviets would not tolerate in Eastern Europe any government which would not submit to communist domination. . . .

Under such circumstances, the hapless Benes and the disheartened leaders of the democratic parties were at the mercy of Stalin. . . .[3]

However, the Soviet and Communist inroads into Czechoslovakia were not unwelcome. Indeed, the same analyst maintained that, in May 1945, the Communists' influence in Czechoslovakia was so strong that there would have been no difficulty in turning the country into a Communist state immediately. The fact that this was not done can be explained by several factors. His explanation is that at the time Stalin was hoping to take over France and Italy by parliamentary means, as they were the countries in which the Communist parties had a large following. 'Since much could still be gained by continued repetition of the wartime tune of allied cooperation, Stalin wished to refrain as much as possible from alarming the Free World.'[4] Other commentators proffer different explanations. Many believe that Stalin was genuinely anxious to maintain the wartime alliance, and refrained from imposing Communist governments on East European countries till such time as the Western powers began to implement anti-Communist measures in West European countries. As all these events happened virtually simultaneously, most historians have found it difficult to establish the cause and the effect, and tend to ascribe the blame either to the American side or to the Soviet side, following their personal inclination.

Whichever version is correct, it must not be forgotten that the new Czechoslovak Communist-dominated government was a voluntary coalition between the government-in-exile in London and the Communist leadership exiled in Moscow. As such, it was unique. Most of the other Bloc countries were ex-enemies and their goverments were constituted under some form of the 'popular front' formula. The two exceptions were Yugoslavia (then still in the Soviet sphere of influence) and Poland: the former produced its own Communist-led government and eliminated the monarchy and the monarchist forces; the latter case was more complicated. The Polish government-in-exile in London split under the pressure to join a Communist-dominated coalition, and though one or two leaders agreed to return to Warsaw, the majority of the government refused to do so. Despite strong pressure, both from the British government and from the Polish Communists, the exiled government persisted in its refusal. The Czechoslovak government, on the other hand, went back voluntarily and hopefully, and thus provided legitimacy for the new authorities. A great many of the future problems were to stem from this fact alone.

The take-over by the Communists in February 1948 has been well documented and will not be commented upon here.[5] It is, however, necessary to review some versions of the take-over, which have emerged at a later stage, as they indicate that the Communists had more support among the population as a whole than had been previously thought. One account states that, during the take-over, large crowds gathered in the central square in Prague to support it, while there was only a small student demonstration against the Communists. In the meantime, Gottwald, Nosek and Zapotocky went to the president's residence to present him with a list of new ministers – all Communists or Communist sympathisers. After an hour of negotiations, with the 'roar of the Communist demonstration in Wenceslas Square clearly audible, the President yielded, accepted the resignations and appointed the new government'. The newly confirmed prime minister, Gottwald, then went directly to the square and 'announced his final victory to the crowd which went hysterical with joy'. Though this was, no doubt, a crowd of Communist supporters, summoned specially for the occasion, the very fact that such a large gathering could be called upon demonstrates that there was a large degree of support for the Communists in Czechoslovakia at this particular time.[6]

The Constitutional Assembly approved the new government by 230 votes out of 300, and Czechoslovakia returned to its former calm; public order was never disturbed 'and not even the United Nations could demonstrate that a violent revolution with Soviet help took place in Czechoslovakia'. The beneficiaries of the take-over were the two major Communist players, Gottwald and Notovny, assisted by the minister of the interior, Nosek. Although Nosek, as minister of the interior, is generally blamed for the 'abuses of Socialist legality', the man in charge of the security forces was Rudolf Slansky. Slansky, perhaps the most intelligent man in the leadership, 'concentrated on matters of national security, though he also convinced his fellow leaders, Gottwald and Zapotocky, of the necessity of economic planning, collectivisation of agriculture and administrative reorganisation'. For a time it seemed that Slansky was in complete control and would compete for power with Gottwald. 'However, on Soviet advice Gottwald swiftly eliminated Slansky, executing him ultimately. . . .'[7]

Slansky himself was, therefore, not entirely innocent of institutionalising terror, even though he later suffered it himself and may have been executed pointlessly. But there is little direct evidence that Slansky's fate was sealed by the Russians. At that stage, Gottwald was intent on securing complete power and wanted to eliminate all those who might have posed a threat. Fourteen officials were tried with Slansky for treason. One of the survivors of the trial, Eugen Loebl, died in 1987. He had been economic adviser to Jan Masaryk, the minister of foreign affairs during and after the Second World War. In 1948 Loebl was appointed First Deputy Minister of Foreign Trade; he was arrested in 1949, and in 1952 was tried together with Slansky and the other accused. 'Eleven were hanged. Mr Loebl and two deputy foreign ministers were sentenced to life imprisonment. After serving eleven years in prison, five in solitary confinement, Mr Loebl was released in 1963.' Following the Warsaw Pact invasion of Czechoslovakia in 1968, Loebl emigrated to the United States and died there, the last surviving victim of the purges in Czechoslovakia.[8]

Such a blood-bath had been unheard of in the history of liberal, democratic Czechoslovakia since its inception, and proves the degree of alarm among some leaders, which could only have been induced by some perceived threat. It also proves that the executions and imprisonment were the work of the Czechoslovak leadership and were not Soviet-inspired. The proof lies partly in the fact that Loebl was not released from prison until ten years after Stalin's death, though in other countries of the Bloc most political prisoners were released immediately. It is clear that the prisoners were a continuing threat to the Czechoslovak leadership, and remained so for some years to come. It later turned out that those who had been executed, the dead, proved to be even more of a threat in the following years. It was almost a case of ghosts of the executed coming back to haunt the living.

If one accepts the hypothesis that Gottwald himself was responsible for the purges and the barbaric treatment of prisoners, then the continuing repression in Czechoslovakia, even after other countries in the Bloc had de-Stalinised, is easier to explain. The leaders could not afford to relax and liberalise because they had too many crimes to account for; any relaxation might bring forward witnesses to their misdeeds. This was even more likely because so many people were involved in the carrying out of the purges. It was noted that:

> Throughout 1952 the party leaders in Czechoslovakia were in a state of excitement. After the mass arrests in 1951 the purge was snowballing into a catastrophe and no one knew whose turn it would be next. Central committee members, ministers, civil servants, security agents, economists, generals and intellectuals were slowly pulled in, each group yielding a given number, as if quotas had been fixed in advance. Then in November 1952 the greatest political trial was staged in which the Secretary-General of the Party, R. Slansky, Foreign Minister, V. Clementis and many others were destroyed . . . the circumstances of their demise were so sordid and such a travesty of justice – the sentences were based on confessions obtained after torture – that even several party leaders were appalled.[9]

At the same time, possibly to avoid further purges or to please the Soviet leadership, the Czechoslovak party began to imitate all the CPSU structures. In 1952 it changed its statutes to comply with Soviet usage. In March 1953 it allowed the title of the party chairman to lapse. This occurred when Gottwald, who bore this title, died. His successor as president of the republic and the head of the party was not given any specific party title. The direction of the work of the secretariat was entrusted to Antonin Novotny, but his position was not regularised until September 1953 when, after Khrushchev was elected First Secretary of the CPSU, Novotny was chosen to fill the same post in the Czechoslovak party.[10] It can be discerned from these changes that there was a continuing and sustained effort to please the Soviet leadership. Since this leadership, after the death of Stalin, was counselling liberalisation and Novotny was a protégé of Khrushchev, the question must be asked: why did the Czechs not liberalise and de-Stalinise in the following period?

It has already been suggested above that the surviving leadership had too much blood on its hands to permit liberalisation. But there were additional reasons. Apparently, an investigation into the abuses in the purge trials was started in January 1955. 'The upshot of this investigation was limited: only a few investigators were dismissed and arrested. . . . On 23 April 1956 the politburo accepted the report of the Commission, but decided to do nothing about it; political upheavals within the Communist orbit were the excuse for inactivity.' But the real reason was different: 'After Stalin's death the Czechoslovak Communist Party and its leaders were in a difficult position concerning the security services. To start with it was impossible to take action against them for they were needed.' There had been mutinies in labour camps attached to the Czech uranium mines (which were deemed to be absolutely necessary for the country's economy), as well as hunger strikes in the largest jails in the country. The secret police cracked down on both movements and proved its usefulness. Finally, 'when in 1957 . . . Novotny became the absolute leader and Gottwald's successor, he resolutely refused to curtail them [police powers] any further, thus making it clear that he would make use of them if special circumstances required it'. It was not until 1957 that some police-men who had committed crimes against humanity were tried and sentenced to long terms of imprisonment; but this only applied to those who had tortured party members. The agents who had tor-tured non-party suspects were either reprimanded or dismissed from service. As a result, apart from a few notorious policemen, the security apparatus remained intact.[11]

When Novotny's new secret police chief, Barak, attempted to get at the truth of past trials, he was purged and sentenced to fifteen years of forced labour in 1962. Judging by all these actions, Novotny was unwilling to dismantle the security apparatus, as had been done in other countries of the Bloc, because he felt he needed it to retain power. He was even a party to new purges: in the 1960s, the security forces staged several mass trials of both Communists and non-Communists.

In 1967 Novotny tried to intimidate restless intellectuals by permitting the security police to stage another public trial of the writer Benes and of several students for subversion and espionage. To save his own position, in December 1967, Novotny was alleged to have ordered the 8th Section chief, Mamula, to prepare lists of factional opponents to be arrested. But by this time, the very security agents refused to move, because they probably came to realise that they would be blamed and suffer for whatever they would do.

It was not until Novotny's fall in 1968 and the installation of Dubcek, that the security police apparatus was dismantled – only to be reconstituted after the removal of the reformist leader.[12]

Judging by all the above events, Novotny's record is very black.

The only justification that can be found for it is the fact that he was tutored in the Stalinist school of government, that he was a follower of Zapotocky and Gottwald, and that he was unable to change his attitudes. In addition, it may be profitable to examine the relationship between the hardline politics of Czechoslovakia and the country's unique situation on the borders of Western Europe, as well as bearing in mind its extensive uranium deposits. The uranium brought in handsome profits to Czechoslovakia, the Soviet Union had embarked on a major programme of rearmament, and the country's geo-political position militated against any liberalisation which might open the doors to the West. In the final analysis, it may eventually be established that Novotny was not to be blamed personally for the policies of terror, but that these were made imperative by a mixture of politics, geography and military pressure. A very similar situation arose again in 1968, when strong reaction to Dubcek's plans to liberalise was re-enacted. This may point to the fact that Moscow objected to a liberal trend in Czechoslovakia under any circumstances, though the implementation of terror was left to the Czechs.

Some commentators have ascribed Novotny's policies to force of circumstances. It has been noted that in all Western accounts, Novotny has been described as 'conservative', 'neo-Stalinist', 'opportunistic', and 'unscrupulous'.

> One may readily concede that compared to the doggedness of the GDR leader Walter Ulbricht or the ability to manoeuvre and compromise of Janos Kadar, Novotny did not really succeed in finding a path between the firmness of the former and the flexibility of the latter. Whether this was because of Novotny's personality or because of the surrounding circumstances does not really concern this study.[13]

However, it is admitted that Novotny's policies were not popular, particularly in relation to the country's economic crisis: 'It would be difficult to argue that the policies of the Novotny Government were accepted with great enthusiasm'.

An interesting theory is developed by the same commentator about the origins of the Czechoslovak economic crisis. According to this, the crisis was not caused by the Czechoslovak government blindly following the centralised Soviet model, but, on the contrary, by a decentralising process which was begun in 1958. As a result of this, the Czechoslovak economy was neither controlled nor co-ordinated. To give but one example, the automobile industry, where car production plants increased their output, did not have a corresponding rise in the production of tyres and glass. If such lack of co-ordination was the case throughout the economy, then Novotny's government stands indicted not only on the grounds of terror, but also on those of economic ignorance and lack of overall direction.

However, Novotny's problems did not end there. He also found real difficulties in dealing with the intellectuals. The post-Stalinist intellectual revival which first occurred in Poland and Hungary spread, at a later stage, to Czechoslovakia. An important landmark was the Kafka Conference which was held in 1964. Among other activities, the intellectuals also made strenuous efforts to rehabilitate the victims of Stalinist trials, beginning in 1963, but without result. However, as the opposition grew in numbers, more blows were struck at Novotny. The Writers' Congress, held in 1967, was an occasion at which speakers made 'massive attacks' on Novotny and this gave a signal to the intellectuals to press for reforms. The condemnations were directed at both Novotny and his government, possibly because 'the confrontation between Novotny and the *literati* occurred because the former, unlike Janos Kadar, was not capable of striking a balance with enlightened intellectualism. Or possibly, the confrontation occurred . . . because the Czech intelligentsia felt alienated on account of receiving neither material nor moral recognition.'[14]

At this juncture, therefore, the picture of Novotny is that of an ageing, inflexible, stubborn and unintellectual man, with strong dictatorial leanings and a very brutal record. This individual was governing a country which was still intimidated, but which felt that the climate in the Bloc had changed. It must have been clear that, despite his past usefulness to Moscow, Novotny had become superfluous. At some point, possibly even before 1968, the decision was made to dispense with him – which he was given to understand by Brezhnev himself. When Novotny complained to the Soviet leader about the Czech dissenters, and asked for his help, Brezhnev said: 'This is your business', and refused to become involved.[15] With the benefit of hindsight, it might have been better for all parties concerned if Brezhnev had become involved at this stage, instead of intervening later when much more serious problems arose. But it was in Brezhnev's nature not to look for trouble, unless the situation threatened the security of the Bloc. This trait has been well demonstrated, and has been strongly condemned by the Gorbachev leadership. Novotny's rule came to an end eventually – at a very inconvenient time for the Soviet leadership. His former protector, Khrushchev, had only been out of power for less than four years, and Khrushchev's successor, Brezhnev, had not yet consolidated his power completely. In the circumstances, Brezhnev was so busy with internal affairs that he had little time to spare for Novotny's problems. Besides, by that time Czechoslovakia had lost some of its strategic and industrial value. Altogether, Brezhnev must have felt that the Czechs could be left to their own devices and that being loyal Communists and reliable allies, they would be able to sort out their own difficulties. Brezhnev was to pay a high price for this neglect.

In some ways, therefore, Novotny was as much a victim of circumstance as Slansky before him, and Dubcek after him. The circumstances were fixed by Czechoslovakia's role in the Bloc, by the Bloc's standing in Europe, and by the Soviet leadership's feeling of insecurity. Just as Khrushchev could not afford to lose grip on Hungary so soon after his accession to power, so Brezhnev, though more secure than Khrushchev, could not afford to relax Soviet power in Czechoslovakia. Even had he wanted to do so, the other leaders in the Bloc, and most notably the East Germans, would not have allowed it. Though Novotny's negative personality played a part in the whole Czechoslovak tragedy, it is difficult to establish how big a part this was. It is quite possible that the situation would have been untenable for any leader, though it must be admitted that Novotny seems to have acted with the utmost ineptitude.

Dubcek, the Prague Spring, the débâcle

Novotny's removal was unlamented, and when he left, the last Stalinist leader was eliminated in Czechoslovakia. But he had left his mark on the country, just as Stalin had left his mark on the Bloc. His refusal to resign for such a long time and his inflexible policies have made the Prague Spring a far more radical event than might have been expected. As a nation, the Czechs do not tend to engage in adventures; on the contrary, they are usually inclined to caution. But the fact that the nation had been constrained for so long, that frustrations had built up among all classes, and that Soviet impatience with Novotny's regime became well known, all helped to exacerbate the situation.

Had Novotny resigned voluntarily at the right juncture, instead of being removed from office after violent scenes, Dubcek would probably have become a moderate reformer, a moderniser in the Kadar mould. As things turned out, the scene was set for a much more dramatic outcome. Although much of the blame must be laid at the door of Brezhnev for having washed his hands of the Czechoslovak turmoil till it was too late to introduce peaceful change, the main problem lay in Novotny's personality. He had antagonised too many people for too long. It was noted that:

> The famous Fourth Writers' Congres of 1967 intensified the debate and, by the end of that year, the pressure on Novotny to resign mounted because he was seen as the main obstacle to reforms. There were fiery confrontations in the Central Committee during its October and November sessions until finally amidst further violent clashes Novotny was replaced as First Secretary by Alexander Dubcek.

Dubcek was considered to be a pro-Soviet official; three years earlier he had been called a 'staunch party apparatchik' by an emigré Czech writer.[16] Despite this, he was thought to be capable of succeeding Novotny, and was acceptable to all sides in the conflict. The reason for this lay not so much in Dubcek's ability to govern, as in the fact that Novotny was by then under fire from all party factions. Virtually all the groupings were intent on removing him. The most important of these were the economists, headed by Ota Sik, who 'could not stand much more of President Novotny's ignorant interference'. The second group consisted of the Slovaks; they were discontented with Prague's domination. The third group was a collection of younger Communist leaders, who were rising in the hierarchy and who despised the 'antiquated methods' of their seniors. One of the leaders in this group was Alexander Dubcek; he had been associated with it since 1963. Novotny must have sensed danger from this direction, for in October 1967, after a shooting incident at the border in which the frontier guards killed several would-be escapees, he made a personal attack on Dubcek, then a Presidium member and the First Secretary of the Slovak Communist Party. He accused him of being a Slovak nationalist, which at that time was a dangerous offence. To Novotny's surprise, only one Presidium member supported him; all the others were indignant at this charge. 'All the others . . . rejected Novotny's allegations, which in the not so distant past meant explusion from the party and imprisonment.'[17]

The crisis came to a head on 19 December 1967 when, during a recess, the opposition discovered that Novotny's security chief, Mamula, had prepared a list of those to be arrested; Dubcek figured on the list. Altogether about one thousand Communist 'radicals' were on it.[18] The president was also said to be ready to use the army against the Central Committee if it voted against him and his faction. Some sources consider these rumours an invention, but they were sufficient to frighten the hesitant members of the Central Committee. The Plenum's preparatory commission voted by nine votes to three to recommend to the Central Committee that the First Secretary be dismissed. On 5 January 1968, the Central Committee met in a plenary session, and Novotny himself announced his resignation as First Secretary, though he retained the title of President of the Republic.[19]

One of the more fascinating factors facilitating Dubcek's accession to power was that he owed it to Novotny's zeal in destroying his rivals. In the early 1960s Novotny suspected that Rudolf Barak, who had chaired the commission of enquiry on the misuse of justice, was a serious contender for power. Barak, by then head of the secret police, had no such designs, having been a low-level official at the time of the purge trials. He saw his new position as chairman of the commission as an opportunity for promotion.

> Novotny, on his part, saw that the only way he could escape an
> untimely end to his political career was to prevent anyone else in the
> leadership from taking the initiative and appearing as a champion of
> the restoration of socialist legality. Rudolf Barak was one such
> potential champion, in fact probably the most dangerous of all to
> Novotny.

Before Barak could proceed with his plan (if there was a plan), Novotny had him stripped of office, expelled from the party, arrested, and tried in camera before a military court in February 1962. The charges included misuse of power and embezzlement. Barak was condemned to a long prison sentence and Novotny gained two advantages: on the one hand he was rid of a potential rival who, because of his key position in the rehabilitation procedure and the popularity the rehabilitation issue enjoyed in wide party circles, might actually have ousted him. On the other hand, Barak served as a convenient scapegoat who could be blamed for all the delays . . . in redressing the past wrongs of political justice.

Novotny then proceeded to appoint a new investigative commission, whose chairman was Drahomir Kolder. One of the members of the commission was Dubcek.[20]

Thus, in trying to eliminate one rival, Novotny prepared the way for another one, and one who proved to be much more dangerous. Dubcek had been born in Slovakia in 1921, the son of a minor official. He became an apprentice machine fitter in 1938, joined the Communist Party in 1939, and worked in the Skoda Works in Dubnica nad Vahom between 1941 and 1945. He took part in the Slovak rising against the Nazis in the autumn of 1944. At the end of the war, he advanced through the party ranks in Slovakia and was eventually seconded to the Party High School in Moscow, where he spent the period between 1953 and 1958. He became the First Secretary of the Slovak Communist Party in April 1963 and was further promoted in January 1968, when he was voted into the office of First Secretary of the Czechoslovak Party.[21]

Judging by his exemplary party career and his rapid promotion in the party ranks, Dubcek must have been considered a loyal ally of the Soviet leadership. Indeed, it is believed that he had considerable influence over the Soviet leaders, and that it was he who persuaded Leonid Brezhnev in December 1967 that neither he, nor his supporters, were either Slovak nationalists or deviationists. It has been said that Brezhnev trusted Dubcek because his Russian language was excellent. Some sources even maintain that Brezhnev and Dubcek worked out a political compromise in September 1967. If this is correct, then it meant that Dubcek was able to offer a strong guarantee that he could deliver a peaceful settlement. It still remains a mystery why such a settlement was not reached, unless Czech frustrations had been mounting too high, or – as the Soviet authorities maintained – external influences prevailed in Prague during the spring of 1968. Nevertheless, throughout the turmoil, and for a long time afterwards, Dubcek remained what he had always been: a faithful party servant, an ally of the Soviet Union, and a confirmed *apparatchik*, albeit of a more modern and humane kind. In retrospect, it can be seen that Dubcek's espousal of liberal causes in 1968 was more connected with his attempts to introduce a federal structure in Czechoslovakia and to provide an economic impetus for the system, than with a desire to introduce parliamentary democracy. Nor was Dubcek a strong champion of the intellectuals. He merely perceived the intellectuals as an important element in the country's revival. Throughout the passage of the Prague Spring, he was never the originator of revolt, merely a man who had been pushed into action – some of which he appeared to dislike – by those behind him and by popular pressure. Though for a time he was the idol of dissident intellectuals, he seldom appeared to be carried away by their revolutionary ideas. If his commitment to 'Communism with a human face' was sincere, his devotion to the socialist cause and to the Soviet Union was not in doubt.

Though Dubcek was acclaimed as a liberator in 1968, he capitulated to Soviet demands as soon as the reform movement began to threaten the Soviet domination of Czechoslovakia. In this respect he resembled his countryman, President Benes, in 1938 much more than the Polish leader, Gomulka, in 1956. While in the Czech case, both decisions may have been more sensible than resistance to overwhelming forces, even a token resistance to the invading Warsaw Pact forces would have been a symbolic gesture, just as resistance in 1938 might have staved off the total collapse of Czechoslovakia, or even – if one dared to hope for it – stopped the outbreak of the Second World War. Dubcek's appeal to the Czechs not to resist may have saved bloodshed; it is questionable whether it saved Czech self-respect. It certainly delayed necessary reforms by some twenty years.

Dubcek's loyalty to the cause of the Bloc brought him reward after he was voted out from his post as First Secretary. Though he had been purged, his next appointment was not too onerous, possibly because, in the wake of the Novotny purges, there was no stomach for more show trials. As early as October 1969, a party journal stated: 'There can be no question of a return to the 1950s, of any kind of revenge.' Dubcek was appointed as ambassador to Turkey in December 1969, and though he was subsequently recalled home and stripped of his party membership, he was not tried for treason as some hardliners had demanded. Instead, he was given a minor post in the Slovak Forestry Commission. Still holding this post, he was even able to carry out minor political propaganda a few years later. In April 1975 it was reported that two documents had received publicity in recent times: 'One was a letter by the deposed party leader, Alexander Dubcek to the Federal Assembly and the Slovak National Council, the other an "open letter" from the Czech playwright Vaclav Havel to the present secretary-general, Gustav Husak.'22

Dubcek's letter, dated 28 October 1974, but not available outside the country till the following spring, when it was smuggled out by a Czech oppositionist, received wide coverage in the West. In the first part of the letter, Dubcek complained about police surveillance of himself and his visitors and claimed that, since his motives were not sinister, there was no need for such surveillance. In the second, much more important part, it addressed the real issues. Dubcek denounced the government at that time, noting that Husak's rule was based on a policy of personal power and that the party ruled by coercion. He maintained that, because of this, a 'web of surveillance and informing' had spread in the country. This had produced an atmosphere of corruption, duplicity, apathy, suspicion and hypocrisy. Dubcek further accused Husak of wrecking Soviet–Czech friendship, rather than – as was being claimed – cementing it. 'Unshaken in his allegiance to the Soviet Union even after his experiences of August 1968, Dubcek reaffirms his conviction that the future of Czechoslovakia can only lie in the community of socialist countries, and in close co-operation with the Soviet Union.' He then returned to the topic of police surveillance and asserted that even the republic's president, Ludvik Svoboda, had the habit of placing transistor radios at his windows, before engaging in any discussions. 'Such precautions speak for themselves and need no comment,' he added.23

Whether by coincidence or not, this letter emerged simultaneously with Havel's letter of protest. Havel, a well-known playwright, had been an advocate of a multi-party system in 1968. He had denounced the August invasion and had called on foreign writers to join in protesting against the aggression. He had also signed the 'Ten Points Manifesto', published on the first anniversary of the invasion, and was eventually indicted for 'preparation of the crime of subversion of the republic'. The trial on this charge never took place, though Havel was interrogated in December 1972, after he had signed a petition to President Svoboda, asking for a Christmas amnesty for political prisoners. Havel, as an outstanding intellectual, felt that literary work in Czechoslovakia was being debased, because the system only allowed conformist writers to publish their work.[24]

On the other side of the fence, Dubcek's successor, Gustav Husak, did not spare his condemnation. In a speech delivered to the joint session of the National Front on 16 April 1975, Husak launched an anti-Dubcek campaign. 'The party leader's speech, delivered in Czech, gave the impression of being at least in part an improvisation and reflected at times his agitation and anger at what he considered to be not only antisocialist activity but even outright treason by Dubcek. . . .'[25] Husak specifically stated that after the death of another outstanding reformer, Jozef Smrkovsky on 14 January 1974, Dubcek had taken over as the leader of a campaign against the system. He further charged that Dubcek had slandered the Soviet Union, that he was a traitor to socialism and a 'lackey' of the bourgeoisie. He called him a counter-revolutionary and reflected bitterly that the treatment meted out to him and his associates had been too mild. He 'devoted some time to what he obviously considered the humane and "political" way the incorrigible reformers of 1968 had been treated. He went on to express doubt whether the "mild treatment" meted out so far had paid off.' He added that the reformers must have decided that the absence of mass arrests and executions was due to stupidity, not to magnanimity; and, finally, suggested that they could leave the country and settle in any bourgeois state of their choice. He then suggested that Olaf Palme, the then Swedish prime minister, who had expressed an interest in Dubcek's letter, can 'have Dubcek tomorrow'.[26]

Dubcek did not emigrate to Sweden, and he was not prosecuted. The political climate in the Bloc had changed so much that such prosecutions were unthinkable. However, Husak may have been too old to realise it at this stage. He probably could not forget the heady days of Gottwald, when rivals and enemies could be disposed of at will. Eventually Dubcek received a measure of revenge over Husak. When Mikhail Gorbachev came to power in the Soviet Union, Husak fell out of favour. On the seventieth anniversary of the Bolshevik revolution Dubcek sent a letter of congratulation to Gorbachev (it was speculated that he might have been acquainted with him during his stay in Moscow), and recalled the reforms introduced in Czechoslovakia in 1968. 'Mr Dubcek's discreet re-entry onto the political scene occurred as the "Prague Spring" . . . was becoming a topic of discussion in the East bloc with Mr Gorbachev's invitation to more open study of Communist history.'[27]

Following the trend of the time, a Soviet party historian told a press conference that the invasion of Czechoslovakia needed to be reconsidered, and a leading Czech dissident noted that: 'If the question is opened, it will open a new situation here. The people who have run this country for nearly 20 years are the men of that intervention. Their only legitimization in power derives from it.' Such unorthodox views were quickly refuted by official Czech sources and the editor of the official newspaper, *Rude Pravo*, commented: 'Our party does not suspect any Soviet of wishing to change the view of 1968.'[28]

A year later, Dubcek was able to express his thoughts more openly; partly because he was allowed to travel abroad, and partly because his old friend, and later his rival, Husak, had been forced to resign as general secretary. In Bologna, the stronghold of Italian Communism where he arrived to be awarded an honorary doctorate in political science, Dubcek asserted that the 1968 reformers had been right: 'I must reaffirm here my clear conviction. Without the external intervention into the affairs of our party and of Czech society, our attempt would have been crowned with success.'[29]

Husak and 'normalisation'

Although Husak was eventually forced to resign his post of general secretary in 1987, his long rule left an imprint on the country, and it was one which was not easy to remove. While Husak did not appear to be a strong personality, and though he was not allowed to use terror, he managed to retain his power for almost twenty years, and even managed to install one of his supporters as his successor. In view of this, it is interesting to look at his background.

Unlike Dubcek and Novotny, Husak had the advantage of a middle-class education. He was born in Bratislava in 1913, attended a high school and completed law studies at the University of Bratislava. He then became a senior official in the Federation of Socialist Academicians in Slovakia. He joined the Communist Party in 1934 and, after the dismemberment of Czechoslovakia, practised as a lawyer in Bratislava from 1938 to 1942. He was arrested several times for illegal activity between 1940 and 1943. However, although he was working in the Communist Party during the war and gaining seniority, he escaped persecution, even though the party was illegal in the puppet republic of Slovakia. He was engaged in partisan activity since 1944 when victory was assured, and after the Soviet armies entered Slovakia continued to be promoted within the party. From December 1944 until February 1945, he spent a year in the Soviet Union, probably on a senior party course.

In 1949 Husak became head of the Slovak Office for Church Affairs and his future seemed assured. However, for the first time in his life, his luck failed him. In February 1951 he was arrested in the second wave of purges and, in April 1954, condemned to life imprisonment as a 'Slovak bourgeois nationalist'. He remained in prison till 1960, becoming a construction worker on his release – employment which he continued until 1963. Considering that he was by then a man of fifty who had never worked as a manual labourer, having always been a professional worker, one is struck by his endurance. He had survived not only the purge, but also the treatment in prison and the hard work that followed.

In 1963 Husak's luck turned again. He was rehabilitated and re-admitted to the party; he became editor of a journal and joined the reformist movement, which, however, he deserted as soon as the intervention in Czechoslovakia threatened. He was rewarded for this by being voted into the office of First Secretary of the Czechoslovak Communist Party in 1969, after the removal of Dubcek. He further strengthened his position by becoming president of the republic in 1975. This post, though honorific, is nonetheless highly coveted in Czechoslovakia.[30]

Although at the outset of his period in office Husak appeared to stand by the ousted Dubcek, he changed his views as he began to consolidate power. Husak managed to run a middle-of-the-road course between the reformists and the hardliners for some time. One commentator noted:

It has always appeared that Husak was a factor of restraint inhibiting the harder-line and more vindictive 'consolidators' who demanded sterner measures against Dubcek and his followers. These were the men who apparently against Husak's wish, had Dubcek recalled from his post as ambassador to Turkey in June 1970.[31]

But later on, as Husak's policies began to falter and his personal popularity reached the lowest levels since Novotny's ratings, he began to feel personal rancour against the ever-popular ousted leader.

Husak's critics maintain that his main flaw was that he craved honours and popularity. He was able to obtain the honours by manipulating the party, but popularity was more difficult to achieve. When the elections for president were held at Prague castle on 29 May 1975, 100 per cent of all deputies voted for Husak. This was not too difficult, however, as Husak was the only candidate for the presidency after General Svoboda resigned or, as some sources suggest, was forced to resign. Following the election, the official eulogist, Alois Indra, who was chairman of the National Assembly, gave a speech full of flattery, and spoke of Husak as the worthy successor of Gottwald, Zapotocky and Svoboda.[32] But the presidential post did not stop criticism and opposition. The opposition came from two sources: the reformers, and the hardliners on the right of the party. This wing became much more powerful in the late 1970s and caused Husak many problems.[33]

Husak felt that he was safely installed in office, even after Gorbachev came to power in the Soviet Union. He refused to compromise on economic reform, telling the Central Committee, 'We will not take the road of any of the market-oriented concepts that would weaken the system of socialist collective property and the party's leading role in the economy. We have had experience with this kind of thing.'[34] Apparently Husak felt that he stood for continuity and loyalty, and thought that Gorbachev would prefer these qualities to the more uncertain ones of the reformists. He had miscalculated. In April 1987 Gorbachev visited Czechoslovakia. By July of the same year the Czechoslovak government had begun to change the country's laws in accordance with Soviet wishes; and towards the end of that year Husak, then almost seventy-five years old, retired as general secretary and was replaced by Milos Jakes.

Jakes was sixty-six years old in 1987 and was clearly a

transitional leader. Not only was he too old for the new model of Gorbachev's leaders, he was also too compromised by his Stalinist past. Since taking office he showed himself to be oppressive in his measures against the intellectuals. Some of the younger reformists will almost certainly come into office, and Jakes will probably not even become the president of the republic.[35] Thus, the wheel will have come full circle since 1968.

Notes

1. Edward Taborsky, *Communism in Czechoslovakia, 1948–1960*, p. 10, quoting Stenographic Reports, 14 December 1938.
2. Taborsky, *Communism*, p. 11.
3. *Ibid.*, pp.14–15.
4. *Ibid.*, p. 16.
5. For a brief account see Olga·A. Narkiewicz, *Marxism and the Reality of Power, 1919–1980*, Chapter 8.
6. J.F.N. Bradley, *Politics in Czechoslovakia, 1945–1971*, pp. 26–7.
7. *Ibid.*, p. 27 and p. 45.
8. 'Eugen Loebl, ex-Prague official, dies', *International Herald Tribune*, 10 August 1987.
9. Bradley, *Politics*, p. 173.
10. Taborsky, *Communism*, pp. 47–8.
11. Bradley, *Politics*, pp. 174–5.
12. *Ibid.*, p. 176.
13. Jürgen Tampke, *The People's Republics of Eastern Europe*, p. 93.
14. *Ibid.*, pp. 97–103.
15. Olga A. Narkiewicz, *Soviet Leaders: From the Cult of Personality to Collective Rule*, pp. 132–3.
16. Tampke, *The People's Republics*, p. 98.
17. Bradley, *Politics*, pp. 181–3.
18. Otto Ulc, *Politics in Czechoslovakia*, as quoted by Bradley, *Politics*, pp. 184–5.
19. Those events have been treated in Narkiewicz, *Eastern Europe*, Chapter 1.
20. Zdenek Suda,. *Zealots and Rebels*, pp. 292–5; see also this chapter, note 12.
21. *Who's Who in Socialist Countries*.
22. RFE Research, *Situation Report*, Czechoslovakia/15, 16 April 1975.
23. *Ibid.*
24. *Ibid.*
25. RFE Research, *Situation Report*, Czechoslovakia/16, 23 April 1975.
26. *Ibid.*

27. 'For Dubcek, a brief brush with politics', *New York Times*, 10 November 1987.
28. *Ibid.*
29. 'Dubcek, in Italy, defends Prague Spring', *International Herald Tribune*, 14 November 1988.
30. See *Who's Who in Socialist Countries* for Husak's biography.
31. RFE Research, *Situation Report*, Czechoslovakia/16.
32. RFE Research, *Situation Report*, Czechoslovakia/22, 4 June 1975.
33. RAD Background Report/123, *Husak in Hradcany Castle*, 6 August 1975.
34. V.V. Kusin, 'Gorbachev and Eastern Europe', *Problems of Communism*, January–February 1986.
35. Richard F. Staar, 'Checklist of Communist parties in 1987', *Problems of Communism*, January–February 1988. Jakes is said to have been responsible for the purge which expelled half a million Communists from the party after the invasion. His official biography can be found in *Pravda*, 18 December 1987. Jakes proved himself to be equally oppressive after his installation as general secretary. In February 1989, the playwright, Vaclav Havel, was condemned to nine months in prison for having taken part in a demonstration on 16 January 1989. About fifty other participants were arrested at the same time. 'Février 1989 dans le monde', *Le Monde*, 12–13 March 1989.

4

The leaders of the German Democratic Republic

Stalinist past, reformist future

Historians sometimes have the unenviable task of writing about nations which may appear perfectly orderly and normal, and then suddenly begin to exhibit manic tendencies – only to return back to normality after a period of time has elapsed. This task is difficult enough, but it is even more difficult to write about the leaders of such nations, for it is necessary to guard against endowing them with the same tendencies that their nations have shown. It is tempting to ignore the manic phases, but a dangerous mistake. Each powerful leader has left an imprint on his country, and, in the case of Germany, Adolf Hitler's influence is clearly still felt more than four decades after his death and the collapse of the Nazi state. Needless to say this chapter does not deal with Nazism or Hitler, but with the German Communist Party, and with the state it set up in parts of Germany after the elimination of Hitler. The influence of Nazism, however, has deeply affected the Communists to an extent that is difficult to envisage.

Hence, when writing about the leaders of the German Communist Party (as it used to be known before its merger with the social democrats), one is confronted by an extraordinary history, set in an extraordinary country, during an extraordinary period, and as a result, one is tempted to endow the leadership with extraordinary capabilities. It is quite true that the early German Communists did have outstanding leaders, Karl Liebknecht and Rosa Luxemburg, for example. But they, together with other able leaders, were executed by nationalist forces during the first round of the German struggle against Communism. The second generation of leaders, of whom the most important was Thaelmann, perished in Nazi concentration camps, or were executed by Stalin. The modern history of German communism only begins with the third generation of leaders. Unfortunately, this generation has turned out to be neither extraordinary nor gifted. Nevertheless, it is striking that these very ordinary people performed very well in a difficult situation, and because of this, they may indeed be described as extraordinary. Such findings alone make it worthwhile to look at their personalities.

The two leaders who were imposed on East Germany after the Second World War, Pieck and Ulbricht, have often been dismissed as Stalin's puppets. It is also usually overlooked that they played a significant role in the difficult task of re-structuring East Germany after the war. When their importance is not in question, they are described as hardline Stalinists. This label fits Pieck, but there is reasonable doubt about Ulbricht. Ulbricht was a more subtle politician than Pieck, often aware of the significance of public opinion, though there were times when he misread it.[1] During the 1953 Berlin workers' uprising Pieck considered that there was no need to take action until the uprising gathered strength; but once he realised that the situation was getting out of hand, he did not hesitate. Thousands of arrests were made, hundreds of activists were tried by special tribunals and executed, and all the Stalinist measures of repression were applied fully. In this respect, therefore, Ulbricht must be considered a Stalinist. The Stalinist mould is also seen at a later stage, when Ulbricht is known to have opposed liberalising measures in other East European countries. However, it is often ignored that Ulbricht was much more pragmatic than his Stalinist image would indicate. When he opposed liberalisation, he usually did so for practical, not ideological, reasons. Sometimes he went out of his way to approve liberal measures – provided these were not described as liberal.

Ulbricht held the position of party leader from 1953 to 1971 – a long period and one which was crucial for the re-building of East Germany and for transforming it into a self-sufficient state, dependent neither on the Soviet Union nor on West Germany. The fact that East Germany became a fairly cohesive nation state, and that it enjoyed a measure of prosperity towards the end of this period, probably says as much for the discipline and hard work of the population as for Ulbricht's pragmatism. However, few analysts would dispute the image of Ulbricht as a party-machine man – a party conceived by the CPSU, and bound by the strict discipline of a disciplined leader. Someone who knew him well in 1970, when Ulbricht was already seventy-seven years old, made the following comment:

> Notwithstanding the liberalizing currents which have made themselves felt in many parts of the Communist world since the death of Stalin, the East German regime of Socialist Unity Party . . , chief, Walter Ulbricht, remains more resolutely Stalinist in its ideological posture and policies, and more impervious to pressures for reform, than almost any other East European Communist leadership.[2]

This commentator, who had been Erich Honecker's personal deputy when the latter was a secretary of the Politburo, reckoned that the first signs of opposition to Ulbricht's autocratic leadership emerged in June 1953, during the Berlin uprising. At this time, several highly placed officials demanded changes in the party structure and wanted to curb Ulbricht's personal domination of the party leadership, in order to mollify the revolutionaries. However, once the uprising was put down, the opposing officials were swiftly purged.

The next wave of opposition occurred in 1956, during the period of the first reforms instituted by Khrushchev. The opposition this time came from the intellectuals. Dr Wolfgang Harich, a professor at Humbolt University and the editor of a party journal, formulated a reform programme. This programme became known as the 'Harich Programme'. It envisaged a policy of 'humanist socialism' and proposed various other reforms, run on the lines of those introduced by the Polish and Hungarian governments. Ulbricht's reaction was swift. Harich was arrested at the end of 1956 and was sentenced the following March to ten years hard labour. Heavy sentences were also given to several of Harich's collaborators. A similar fate befell another academic, Professor Havemann, who gave a series of lectures on the need for reforms in 1963. He was dismissed from his post, expelled from the Academy of Sciences and from the party. At a later date, his sons were arrested for organising demonstrations supporting the Czechoslovak reform movement.[3]

In view of the swift retribution awaiting anyone who opposed Ulbricht, it is not surprising that political opposition was both limited and weak. Ulbricht's autocratic attitudes were not limited to the persecution of opponents; it is believed that the construction of the Berlin Wall in 1961 was on his own initiative. When faced with a drain of highly skilled professionals from the Democratic Republic (estimates differ, but some reliable sources consider that 200,000 people escaped in 1960, and 207,000 in the first six months of 1961), Ulbricht took the drastic step of building a wall between the Eastern and Western sectors of Berlin, in order to stop the exodus. This action, which antagonised both the West and East German populations, appeared to be a typically Stalinist solution. However, it worked after a fashion, though an observer might think that similar results could have been obtained in a more subtle and less dramatic fashion. The Berlin Wall has since become a symbol of Communist oppression and a focal point of Western disapproval.

Even Mikhail Gorbachev, popular though he is in the West, cannot escape the Wall's significance. On the eve of his first visit to the United States, Gorbachev was asked about the Wall in an interview he gave to an American television network.[4] While he managed to turn the question round with his usual mental agility, he was clearly discomfited by it. Gorbachev is a modern, subtle politician, who well understands the value of symbols. Ulbricht was not subtle, and what is more, did not consider matters outside his own sphere of influence of much import. He also tended to show complete contempt for anyone whose views differed from his own. It is possible that the long period of time he had spent in Stalinist Moscow, combined with his advanced age, made him more rigid than would otherwise have been the case.

Yet, although narrow-minded and rigid in the political sphere, Ulbricht was not averse to experimentation with economic and technological reform. The economic policies which East Germany pursued during his period in office made the country into one of the most prosperous in the Bloc. The reforms put into operation from 1963 onwards transformed East Germany into an advanced industrial society, and even though their substance cannot be attributed to Ulbricht, his merit lay in encouraging them, and in giving the technocrats the power to extend them as far as they deemed necessary.[5]

Erich Honecker: the technocratic reformer

Though Ulbricht ruled autocratically, he was not unmindful of the need for an orderly succession. Bearing this in mind, he had been grooming his successor for several years. Erich Honecker had been described as a 'dogmatist' in 1970, before succeeding to the top post. He had risen through political expertise, not through technocracy, and had headed that faction of the Politburo which was said to favour the demands of stability above those of modernisation. It was thought that his group tended to be older and less well-educated than the technocrats. On the face of it, Honecker appeared to be yet another *apparatchik*: disciplined, loyal, obedient and hard-working. But behind this drab façade lay not only an interesting and unusual history, but also an intelligent and sensitive man.

Honecker's West German friend, the prime minister of Saarland, Oskar Lafontaine, has remarked that the Saarlanders are survivors, not heroes. 'Nothing about Honecker is spectacular,' he remarked. 'But Honecker's survival *is* spectacular,' a commentator noted. 'Like the creatures of the Galapagos Islands, he has survived evolutionary laws that long ago condemned others of his kind. He is a living fossil from the great socialist and working-class movements of the turn-of-the-century Germany.'[6]

Erich Honecker was born in 1912 in Neunkirchen, a mining village in Saarland. His father, a miner, was a social democrat, but joined the German Communist Party when it was formed in 1919. Young Erich was brought up, together with his brothers and sisters, to be atheistic and anti-nationalist. Despite this, one of his brothers joined the Hitler Youth after the Nazi take-over of power. But Erich, after joining the Young Pioneers at the age of ten, never forsook socialism. In 1926 he became a member of the Communist Youth League, and in 1929, when he was old enough, he joined the KDP (Kommunistische Partei Deutschlands). He was sent on a course for youth organisers at the Lenin School in Moscow in 1930, and became the secretary of the Saarland Communist youth organisation in 1931. Among his other activities at this time, he had trained as a roof-maker, a skill which was to prove of great value in the future.

Because of its special post-Versailles status, Saarland was less constrained than the rest of Germany following the Nazi take-over of power in 1933. However, Honecker did not stay in the region; he was being used on missions for the party all over Germany, and it was during one of these that he and several other Communists were arrested on their return from abroad. Even this worked to Honecker's advantage, because he was arrested in 1935, before the worst Nazi terror started, and in 1937 he was sentenced to ten years imprisonment by a regular court. Thanks to this sentence, he was sent, not to a concentration camp, but to a prison in Bradenburg-Gorden where the guards were regular prison wardens, not Nazi guards. It was here that his trade proved useful; he was a model prisoner and soon became 'trusty', being allowed out of prison to work as a roofer. There is some doubt about the actual date of his liberation. According to his official biography, he was liberated from prison in 1945 when the Red Army arrived; but his main biographer states that he absconded from prison some two to three weeks before the liberation and went to stay with friends in the neighbourhood. Some biographers state that the summary executions which took place in prison before the arrival of the Red Army horrified him, and that he has been haunted by the spectre of his fellow-prisoners being executed ever since. His experiences in prison are said to have convinced him even more strongly of the necessity for introducing socialism into Germany.

It is a matter of interest that Honecker was in the same prison as Robert Havemann, whom he later persecuted for his 'Eurocommunist' views; some biographers believe that it was during this period that he acquired a distrust for intellectuals. However, it would appear that Honecker and Havemann had nothing in common, apart from the fact that they were both Communist prisoners. Honecker was not an intellectual; his education was minimal, and he was an artisan by profession. This fact alone would have made a lot of difference in Germany, even in the Communist Party. Though prisons are great levellers, it is unlikely that Honecker and Havemann would have become bosom friends. Moreover, Honecker was never greatly admired by men. Lippmann notes that when he was young, men found him distant and supercilious, while women found him pleasant and even fascinating. One biographer noted that, when young, Honecker was 'quite good looking'.

After the liberation, Honecker became the head of the Free German Youth and moulded it into a Communist organisation. He became a candidate member of the Politburo in 1950, was sent on a party course to Moscow in the period 1956–7, and became secretary of the Central Committee of the United Socialist Party (the SED), in 1958; simultaneously, he was made a full member of the Politburo. In 1971 he succeeded Ulbricht as First Secretary of the SED.[7]

Honecker's progress seemed assured after 1945, and his official life easy. But this was not really the case. In the first instance, Honecker had to carry out all the very difficult tasks of this period; he also had to obey Ulbricht implicitly. As noted above, anyone who disagreed with Ulbricht was instantly dismissed; Honecker, however, survived, perhaps because he had an instinct for obedience. He also had to cope with difficult personal problems. In 1947 he had married his deputy in the youth organisation, Edith Baumann, but two years later met Margot Feist and left his wife to live with her. His first wife initially refused him a divorce, only agreeing when pressed to do so by Pieck and Ulbricht. These two leaders were worried because Honecker's irregular life-style was creating a scandal in party circles. Honecker's divorce came through in 1953 and he married Margot Feist. There was a daughter by the first marriage, and another one by the second. However, his second marriage proved no more successful than the first.

Margot Feist is the daughter of a Halle Communist. She was born in 1927 and after the Second World War became co-founder of the Halle Anti-Fascist League. She joined the Communist Party in 1945 and transferred to the SED after its formation. Because of her association with Honecker, she was transferred from Halle to Berlin in 1950, where she worked with him very closely in the secretariat of the Central Committee. In 1987 she was described as a handsome woman 'with a purple hair rinse'; but also a woman whose marriage had failed. She was at that time minister of education, a post for which she was qualified on merit because of her reputation as an efficient and reasonable manager. During the period when she worked with Honecker, she was highly praised:

> Her combination of intelligence and warm cordiality is appealing. Functionaries who hesitated to turn directly to Honecker would come to her with their problems. . . . How much of a moderating influence she still exerts over the sometimes irascible Honecker is uncertain. In well-informed circles of East Berlin . . . the rumor persists that they have been separated for a long time.[8]

One is thus presented with two, if not three, different images of Honecker: a convinced socialist from childhood, a model prisoner in Nazi Germany, and – finally – a survivor, who managed to avoid being executed in a Nazi prison. He can also be seen as a tireless worker, a loyal assistant to Ulbricht, and the official who was entrusted with the task of building the Berlin Wall. He acquired the reputation of a consistent and reliable worker. That, at least, is the picture which is presented to the outside world. But in private life, there is another Honecker: a man who charmed women; who embarked on two marriages, both of which ended badly; and eventually, an old man, homesick for his native Saarland. There is also the irritable Honecker, unapproachable by his subordinates. And there is the warm and homely Honecker, who imports wine and beer from his homeland, which he has not seen for decades. Which of these is the real Honecker? It is difficult to decide. But he is certainly not the mediocre, colourless bureaucrat, as he is often pictured: 'In general, Honecker fits the stereotype of the colorless, disciplined and cautious party bureaucrat, who has little understanding of the "new economics", and who has never displayed much initiative in the area of policy-making.'9

The opposite is probably true. Since replacing Ulbricht as First Secretary, Honecker has continued the policy of stability; but he has also considerably expanded the technological potential of the country. Second, he has pursued an original and skilful foreign policy, while managing to remain loyal to the CPSU and conforming to the theory of socialist internationalism. This, in itself, is an achievement. On the other hand, he has shown a great deal of anger and irritability when confronted with any kind of dissent, even when it comes from former prison inmates. In 1979 he threatend to pass a law which would carry a five-year prison sentence for German writers who published their works abroad. This produced protests from within the party: 'Earlier this year, several East German writers sent private letters to . . . Erich Honecker, protesting at the treatment of the dissident philosopher, Robert Havemann, and the author, Stefan Heym. These writers are now faced with the choice of either having their works unpublished or being sent to prison for publishing them in the West,' commented one analyst.10 A decade later, things were no different. This led one film director to make a film about a dissenting East German writer who was given a one-way visa to West Germany to make sure he·could not return.11

However, while pursuing a hard line with intellectuals at home, Honecker displayed a great deal of flexibility abroad. His attitudes towards the Federal Republic have been described as a 'double-track' approach. He made it clear that he would continue and intensify Ulbricht's policy of 'demarcation', while, on the other hand, attempting to facilitate a *rapprochement* with West Germany, 'either because of a pragmatic reassessment of East German interests, or because of Soviet pressures, or because of both.'[12]

One is thus presented with yet another face of Honecker: that of professional 'political specialist', who established a reputation for organisational ability in the early period from 1946 to 1955. In this period, as secretary for security affairs in the Central Committee, he became an expert on all questions dealing with party organisation, control and security. But Honecker is not just another ex-secret policeman: he kept in touch with the needs of the people, and took pains to

> increase domestic political stability by taking steps to improve the morale of the East German people. The most important feature of the Honecker course in this respect is a planned rise in the living standards of the population. . . . Possibly this stress on meeting the people's needs was triggered . . . by the widening gap between the living standards of the GDR and those of the FRG.[13]

Despite oppressive measures at home, Honecker improved his international standing considerably. He had been on friendly terms with Leonid Brezhnev, and, despite the generation gap, got on well with Mikhail Gorbachev. His relations with the West German leaders became almost warm, though much of the credit for this goes to the West German social democrat leaders, Willy Brandt and Helmut Schmidt. Honecker and Schmidt first met in Helsinki during the signing of the Accords in 1975. Since then, Mr Schmidt has had formal summit meetings with all the other Communist Bloc leaders, and established particularly warm links with Poland's Edward Gierek, 'but, until late last year, always avoided a meeting with Mr Honecker'. One of the reasons for this reluctance was the East German's desire to hold the meeting in East Berlin, which would legitimise the status of the German Democratic Republic, and of Berlin as its capital. Eventually, Schmidt agreed to meet Honecker in 1979, but as soon as the announcement was made, Soviet forces invaded Afghanistan. American pressure is assumed to have been behind West Germany's cancellation. The meeting was finally arranged at the end of August 1980, but not in East Berlin. It was held in the Rostock region and the discussions centred on economic ties.[14]

Honecker has kept up his links with Saarland as far as possible. He is friendly with Oskar Lafontaine, the left-wing social democrat prime minister, who has become a privileged visitor to East Berlin, sipping Saar wine with Honecker deep into the night. According to friends and relatives, Honecker has always been homesick. In 1977, when he gave his first interview to a Western publication, he invited a childhood friend, who was then a journalist for a local Saarland paper, to come to East Berlin. In 1973, two years after coming to power, he met in East Berlin 'a Communist-oriented marching band from Wiebelskirchen in which he had played the drums during the violent days when Communists and Nazis battled on the streets before Hitler's take-over'. One participant in the visit said that Honecker still spoke with a local dialect.[15]

Honecker had been planning to visit his homeland for several years. In 1983 he had to cancel his plans because of the Soviet propaganda campaign against the deployment of American medium-range missiles in Western Europe. 'His most dramatic showdown with Moscow came in September 1984, when he had to call off a visit just three weeks before it was to take place.' Finally, he managed to arrange a visit in September 1987.[16] This visit proved to be a landmark in East–West relations, even though it was not very popular among the local people. The local Social Democratic Party's chairman said: 'The wall separates a lot, and he will be seen as the man who tolerates the wall and then orders to shoot anyone crossing it. There is a certain inhibition toward him.'[17]

The historic visit and its consequences

In 1987, Honecker, by then seventy-four years of age, was planning his long-postponed vist to his native Saarland. He planned to visit his home town, Wiebelskirchen, where his sister, Gertrud Hopp-stadter, still lives in the house where he grew up.

The modest, pale-green house on Kuchenbergerstrasse, where Erich

> Honecker grew up in the 1920s, was freshly painted three years ago,
> when it looked as though the leader of the German Democratic
> Republic would be making a landmark visit to West Germany.
> Perhaps for reasons of frugality, or perhaps out of superstition . . . his
> sister and the sole occupant of the house has decided not to have it
> painted this time.[18]

Despite his advanced age, Honecker travelled a lot in the period
preceding his visit to West Germany. He had visited all the East
European countries, including Romania, and had made a series of
visits to other foreign countries. He seems to have been a popular
guest. His biographer, by no means an admirer, stated that 'Honecker appears less aloof than Ulbricht, more capable of genuine
personal friendships, and more considerate of his subordinates.
These qualities have earned him greater personal popularity, but
by the same token . . . Honecker runs far greater risk of becoming
enmeshed in a political clique composed of his own personal
friends within the ruling élite.'[19]

While Honecker's relations with Helmut Schmidt may have
been slightly strained on a series of subjects (not least, perhaps,
because of bitter memories of the Communist/socialist split in the
early 1930s, which has not yet healed), he made good friends with
the next German chancellor, Helmut Kohl, whom he had first met
in Moscow at Chernenko's funeral. They held a meeting at a guest
house in the Lenin Hills, which lasted more than two hours, where
they are said to have discussed the question of relations between
the two Germanies in all their aspects. In a joint statement, released after the meeting, the two leaders suggested that a new era
of East–West relations was about to begin, and they pledged to
develop 'normal and good relations' between their countries.[20]

Thus the groundwork for Honecker's visit to West Germany
under a conservative leader was laid down long before the visit
occurred. Honecker had prepared the meeting carefully, and what
emerged during his visit, while not a total surprise, was quite revealing. It had already been mooted that an announcement was
being prepared during the visit to the Soviet Union in July 1987 of
the West German president, Richard Weizsacker. At a dinner
given in his honour by the Soviet president, Andrei Gromyko,
Weizsacker stated in his speech: 'It is not always pleasant to recall
embarrassing realities, but neither will they disappear if they are
denied.' He continued: 'The Germans who today live separated in

East and West . . . have not ceased to feel that they belong to one nation, nor will they do so.' He then added that while West Germany would not violate the existing borders, it would aim at removing their divisive and inhumane character.[21]

Implicitly, the West Germans recognised the legitimacy of East Germany. Explicit proof of this was given when Honecker arrived in Bonn at the beginning of September 1987. He was greeted like a head of state, with East German flags flying and the East German anthem being played, even though the Federal Republic does not recognise the Democratic Republic as a foreign state. In his after-dinner speech, Chancellor Kohl announced that West Germany would continue to seek German reunification, adding, however, that the subject 'is at present not on the agenda of world history'. At the same dinner Honecker replied that the reality was to recognise the existence of two independent and sovereign German states.[22] On the following day, a joint statement was released, and it confirmed that the differences between the two states were not resolved, but that each of them would respect the other's independence. Honecker invited Kohl to visit East Germany, and Kohl accepted the invitation. The official part of the visit ended with the signing of various trade, travel and exchange agreements, and both leaders reaffirmed their stand on the position of their respective states.

It was not until Honecker began the unofficial part of his visit, when he was in his own region, that he dropped the bombshell. In the townhall of Neunkirchen he said that if both Germanies worked together and demonstrated further peaceful co-operation, 'then the day will come when the borders will no longer divide us, but when they will unite us. . .'. Qualifying the statement, he added that they would be united 'as the border between the German Democratic Republic and the People's Republic of Poland unites us'.[23] Honecker also predicted that the day would come when free travel, free association and free trade would be conducted normally between the two Germanies. The speech was much more revealing than expected, but in some ways was an apology for the maintenance of the Berlin Wall. The Wall is something of an embarrassment to Honecker, but he has no intention of demolishing it, as long as it serves his purpose, any more than he wants to unify Germany as a capitalist country. Kohl, on the other hand, has a legal obligation to seek reunification, and has to press this point openly. As a result, Honecker can promise a lot, and give away little. Kohl has to demand a lot, and probably hope that he will not get it. He well realises, as he himself has said, that the realities of global politics do not allow for a unified Germany for a long time to come.

Although Honecker did not officially press for the reunification of Germany by force, neither did he give up hope of arranging it by indirect methods. His desire to return to his own homeland may have had a lot to do with the changed attitudes of East Germany. As a Saarlander, a master in the art of survival, and a skilful politician, Honecker knew how to play on the heart-strings of his fellow compatriots. His sentimental return to his home town, the visit to his parents' graves, the joke Lafontaine made about Honecker being the ruler of Prussia, all made it plain that there was more to this visit than a simple state occasion.[24] If a measure of unification is achieved over the next few years, a great deal of credit would have to go to the Communist from the Saarland, who could never forget his home town.

Naturally, Honecker's impact on West Germany did not please everybody. His small stature was compared to Kohl's towering figure, as the small size of East Germany was compared to the large size of West Germany. 'Performance apart, there has never been any doubt which Germany could more easily digest the other,' commented an observer, who clearly forgot his German history.[25] If Prussia could dominate the rest of Germany in the nineteenth century, it could do so again in the future. But clearly, Honecker will not be the new Bismarck. He is too old and he will have to leave office soon, even though at the moment there is no clear-cut successor. For though Honecker's kind of discipline and autocracy has become outdated in the current period, his long term in office and his influence have made him a landmark in the Socialist Bloc's history. This, added to East Germany's economic success story, will make Honecker a difficult act to follow.[26]

Notes

1. See Fejto, *A History*, p. 36, for one such error. When the Berlin workers rose up and went onto the streets on 16 June 1953 to protest at changes in work practices, 'Ulbricht did not take the movement

too seriously; he thought he knew "his" Berliners. "It's raining", he said. "People will go home." ' By the time he realised the seriousness of the situation, it was too late and the uprising grew in strength.

2. Heinz Lippmann, 'The limits of reform Communism', *Problems of Communism*, May–June 1970. For an earlier biography of Ulbricht, see Carola Stern, *Ulbricht: a political biography*, translated from the German.
3. Lippmann, *The Limits*.
4. NBC Television, 30 November 1987.
5. Numbers of escapees as given by Tampke, *The People's Republics*, p. 69. On East German economy, see Narkiewicz, *Eastern Europe*, Chapter 2.
6. 'The survivor who became a fossil, *The Observer*, 6 September 1987.
7. The information was compiled from Heinz Lippmann, *Honecker – Porträt eines Nachfolgers, Who's Who in the Socialist Countries*, and *The Survivor*.
8. Lippmann, *Honecker*, pp. 149–50, in the English translation.
9. Peter C. Ludz, 'The SED leadership in transition', *Problems of Communism*, May–June 1970.
10. 'Writers get jail threat', *The Observer*, 5 August 1979.
11. 'Film: from Germany, "Singing the blues in red"', *New York Times*, 29 January 1988.
12. Peter C. Ludz, 'Continuity and change since Ulbricht', *Problems of Communism*, March–April 1972.
13. Ludz, 'Continuity'.
14. 'Schmidt hopes for gains in summits with East', *The Guardian*, 5 August 1980, and 'Schmidt, Honecker fix date for talks', *Financial Times*, 4 August 1980.
15. 'Saar awaits homecoming of a nostalgic Honecker', *International Herald Tribune*, 5 August 1987.
16. 'Honecker wins approval for "historic" Bonn visit', *International Herald Tribune*, 17 July 1987.
17. 'Saar awaits'.
18. *Ibid.*
19. Quoted by the reviewer of the German version of Lippmann's biography of Honecker. See Melvin Croan, 'Ostpolitik–Westpolitik', *Problems of Communism*, May–June 1973.
20. V.V. Kusin, 'Gorbachev and Eastern Europe', *Problems of Communism*, January–February 1986.
21. 'West German president in Moscow, emphasizes goal of reunification', *International Herald Tribune*, 7 July 1987.
22. 'Honecker starts his historic visit to West Germany', *International Herald Tribune*, 8 September 1987.
23. 'Honecker foresees open German border', *International Herald Tribune*, 11 September 1987.
24. 'East's little big man keeps straight face', *The Observer*, 13 September 1987. Oskar Lafontaine, greeting Honecker, joked that no one

would have guessed that one day the Saar would send its master roof-maker to become a ruler of Prussia.

25. 'East's little big man'.

26. 'East Germany: feeling ill but fearing the medicine', *International Herald Tribune*, 17 June 1988, and 'Is East Germany's record proof that Communist virtues are German?', *International Herald Tribune*, 14 March 1989.

5

Revolution, repression, reform

The Hungarian labyrinth

Hungary is usually described as an East European or Balkan country. Although on the face of it this is a correct designation, it would be a mistake to treat it as a typical East European state. In a unique way Hungary straddles the East and the West, without belonging totally to either. Moreover, as a nation, the Hungarians do not belong to any of the major ethnic groups in the region, being of Ugro-Finnish origin, and they speak a language which is related to that of their Finnish cousins in Northern Europe. To elaborate further, Hungary has had a turbulent history since the Hungarians settled on its territory, and, owing to its geographical situation, the country has seldom enjoyed a sustained period of peace. Finally, the long association with Austria and the Habsburg dynasty, though not popular while it lasted, has made the Hungarians lean towards German-speaking countries, rather than towards the East or the South, for their international contacts.

If the geo-political situation of Hungary is unique, so is its economy. While Hungary has been considered an agricultural country, and sometimes an underdeveloped one, its climate and its vast plains have made it eminently suitable for viticulture and the breeding of fine horses. Owing to this, Hungary has become famous for its wine and its stud farms – luxury items, seldom produced in backward areas. Although this increased Hungary's Western orientation, it also led to a Communist revolution, caused, at least in part, by the influence of large estates and landowners, who held the people in a semi-feudal state of bondage. Because of its revolution Hungary was the only state, apart from the Soviet Union, to have a Communist government for any length of time after the end of the First World War. The Communist government of Bela Kun was eventually overthrown with the help of foreign intervention; the country thus had a recollection of the 'red' terror during Bela Kun's period, and of the 'white' terror which followed it.

In yet another paradox, this land-locked country then proceeded to install an admiral of the fleet as Regent, and set up a monarchy without a monarch. The regime of Admiral Horthy persecuted Communists, and as a result, their numbers were relatively small. When the Nazis occupied the Balkans during the Second World War, Hungary was drawn into the war against the USSR, which provided yet another dilemma for the small Hungarian Communist Party. An earlier problem had been caused by the Soviet–German agreement in 1939: 'The Russo-German Nonaggression Pact of August 1939 gave new cause for consternation and ideological confusion among the rank and file. It was followed in September by the restoration of diplomatic relations between Moscow and Budapest.' A year later, the two governments negotiated a settlement to exchange Hungarian flags captured by the Tsarist forces in 1849 for the most prominent Communists imprisoned in Hungarian jails, Rakosi and Vas. Rakosi had spent a long period of time in Hungarian jails, which could not have been pleasant. On the other hand, it may well have saved his life, for he avoided the purges of Hungarian Communists carried out by Stalin, during which Bela Kun and many other Hungarians were executed. The final irony of the situation was that Bela Kun had arranged for Rakosi – who had by then acquired the status of a martyr – to be reinstated in the party (he had been expelled during the purges), and was himself then executed as a traitor.

It was as a result of these dramatic events that:

> on 1 November 1940 the remnants of the Hungarian colony gathered at Moscow's Kiev Station to welcome the liberated Rakosi and Vas. Rakosi had learned in prison of Kun's arrest, but he was appalled to discover how few of the party's activists had survived. 'The whole party has fallen apart,' he complained almost in tears. 'We have to begin rebuilding from scratch. And with what? Fifty people, if that many . . .'.[1]

In Moscow, Rakosi was not considered a suitable leader to carry out the party's reconstruction; it was rumoured that Stalin did not think much of him, and even considered him a British agent because he had lived in England for a period of time before the First World War. To make things worse, the outbreak of war between Germany and the Soviet Union started a new wave of arrests of Hungarian Communists, now considered unreliable because their country had allied with Germany. This was yet another paradox, and one eye-witness recalls that 'the blow . . . struck all the Hungarian communists. We all felt that our love and loyalty for the Soviet Union . . . had again been unthinkably mocked.' Fortunately for the Hungarians, most of them were soon released, apparently because Rakosi, who, until then, had not defended a single accused Communist, became alarmed and intervened on their behalf.

The task of rebuilding the party was entrusted to Rakosi and Gero, an experienced Comintern agent. For Gero, 'Stalinist orthodoxy was absolute'. When the Hungarians began to argue over the quality of Soviet broadcasts to Hungary, the people who argued were accused of anti-Soviet sabotage, and replaced. Gero also insisted that a major project which was undertaken, that of the translation of the Stalinist history of the CPSU, could not have a single word changed, and even the word order had to be retained. For several years, the Hungarian party had dual leadership, and the question of who would emerge as the single leader was not resolved. Rakosi's reappearance had dashed Gero's hopes of leadership, but the news that Rakosi had won did not become clear for some time. Rakosi's victory was finally announced during the celebration of his fiftieth birthday in March 1942. The celebration was held in Ufa, where the leading members of the Hungarian Communist Party had been evacuated during the German advance on Moscow. At the party Gero raised a toast to Rakosi and indicated that he had been chosen as the new leader.[2]

This account of how Rakosi came to power merely underlines the extreme difficulties under which the Hungarian party had to work in exile. In this period, purges, arrests and executions were commonplace. Although the party was supposed to be undergoing 'reconstruction', it was left without a leader for a considerable period of time. At this stage, the Germans were still theoretically capable of winning the war in the East. In the event of a German victory, the party would be free of the Stalinist terror, but would face persecution from the Nazis and from the pro-Nazi Hungarian government. And, of course, there was always the internal infighting to be reckoned with. The party faced danger on all fronts: should the Germans win the war, the Communists would face certain death; should they lose, Stalin could begin yet another purge; and, in the mean time, each of the Hungarian comrades was ready to denounce the others, should the occasion arise. Taken as a whole, the history of the Hungarian Communist Party was one of fear, exile, treachery and defeat. In view of this, it is perhaps not surprising that when they were finally in power in their own country, the Hungarian leaders retained the previous pattern of action and behaved as though nothing had changed.

There were also other problems. The main one was that the Hungarians were hardly masters in their own house; they were forced to follow Moscow's instructions very strictly. It was noted that:

> whatever the advantages and disadvantages of a command-planning apparatus, Hungary had little choice in the matter prior to the era of de-Stalinization. A non-Marxist–Leninist path was surely impossible for the little country that had fought on the side of the Germans against the Soviet Union during the war and was under occupation by the Red Army.[3]

Even the very return of the Communist leaders was fraught with difficulties. The Red Army reached Hungary before the Allied victory was assured, and the Hungarians were pressed to join the war effort against the Germans. It thus happened that while the Soviet foreign minister, Molotov, was holding discussions with the armistice commission in Moscow, the exiled Communists were despatched homewards. They reached Szeged in mid-October 1944, and issued the party's first newspaper. The advance party consisted of Vas and some minor functionaries. In early November, Gero, Revai, Farkas and Imre Nagy arrived, and Vas was told that these four would set up the new leadership. On 20 November, Rakosi telephoned from Moscow to say that the party's programme had been approved and that the negotiations with the armistice commission had been broken off. The former government was thus ousted without ceremony, and there was every sign that Soviet victory was assured at this point. The news may have been welcome, but was of little consolation to Vas, who had counted on a leadership post.[4]

Eventually, Rakosi arrived from Moscow and set up a coalition government. Some observers believe that Stalin's biggest mistake in Hungary was the appointment of Matyas Rakosi as the leader. Rakosi had been a close collaborator of Bela Kun during the Hungarian revolution, and was ready to use terror at the slightest provocation. 'The Hungarian tragedy can to a large extent be blamed on Matyas Rakosi – the most hated of all Stalin's lieutenants – who, according to his own close associates, was obsessed with the idea of repression.'[5] One has no way of knowing whether any other leader would have proceeded differently, but the accounts of the Hungarian purge trials (if true – and they appear to be) witness a history not only of repression and cruelty, but of extraordinary deviousness. There is an account of how Rajk was induced to confess to his supposed crimes. In order to make Rajk confess, Rakosi is said to have sent Kadar to see him and to promise him anonymous exile in the Soviet Union should he admit to his crimes. In another account, the president of the republic, Szakasists, was handed a confession to sign during a dinner he was having with Rakosi. He was asked to confess that he had been a Gestapo agent and a British spy. ' "If you sign it", said Rakosi, "your fate will be that of Zoltan Tildy. If you refuse, it will be that of Rajk." (Tildy was under house arrest.) Szakasists was thereupon taken away by Gabor Peter and tortured until he signed.'[6]

The purges continued and the whole pre-war generation of home-based Communists was affected by them. All of them were the participants of the 1919 revolution, veterans of the Spanish Civil War, and all were suspected of pro-Western sympathies. Kadar, the most prominment of the home-based Communists, was arrested in April 1951, on charges of treason and espionage. After his experiences in prison, he is reported to have said that 'prisons under Horthy and the Gestapo were bad enough, but they were nothing compared to what one suffered in Rakosi's jails'. In the end, Kadar and all those arrested with him confessed; Kadar received a light sentence of four years; two others were given death sentences, later commuted, and one of the accused killed his family and committed suicide. As the news became known, one of the participants said 'no one would discuss this tragedy. People withdrew into themselves; everyone was left alone with his doubts.'[7]

Although he was hated by everyone and the Russians decided that he must leave, Rakosi would not resign voluntarily, and was finally forced to do so. Mikoyan and Suslov arrived in Budapest on 17 July 1956, and, presumably in response to their pressure, Rakosi handed in his resignation. However, his successor was none other than Erno Gero, well known as a convinced Stalinist. This outcome antagonised the liberals, who were led by Imre Nagy. To compensate for the choice of Gero, some centrists, Janos Kadar, Gyorgy Marosan and Karoly Kiss were appointed to the Politburo. Gero was Mikoyan's protégé and relied on his support. Because of this, the opposition concentrated within the group led by Nagy, who had acquired a reputation as a patriot and a liberaliser. Kadar was hesitant on which course of action to take:

> Kadar, like Ochab in Poland, might have built a bridge between the party and Nagy, but he shared the suspicions of Nagy . . . and especially of his entourage of revisionist intellectuals. Kadar probably thought himself better suited than the former Prime Minister to put Khrushchev's ideas into practice.

Like all of this confused period, this information is somewhat contradicted by another account. According to this, the Soviet leaders, Khrushchev, Malenkov and Molotov, came to Budapest twice, and it was during their second visit, on 27 and 28 June 1956, that Rakosi resigned and delivered a speech confessing his mistakes. Then the 'June resolutions' drafted by Nagy were adopted, and Nagy was nominated for the prime minister's post, while Rakosi retained the post of First Secretary.

> The flouting of socialist legality demanded a sacrifice, and Farkas was momentarily dropped from the Politburo along with Revai and four other members. The truncated Politburo now included Rakosi, Gero, Apro, Hegedus and four other members. After a brief premiership, Nagy was replaced by Kadar on Mikoyan's and Suslov's orders.[8]

Nagy: liberalism and loyalty

Nagy's tenure of office was so brief, compared to that of Rakosi before him and Kadar after him, that not too much attention is paid to his personality, though he is generally described as a 'liberal'. Fejto, who wrote a eulogistic introduction to Nagy's work on 'humanist Communism', maintains that he was a cautious reformer and a conciliator; a man who was caught between the Hungarian people and the Soviet Union, between Communism and democracy; and, finally, a man who became a symbol of the insurrection *malgré soi.*[9]

According to this account, Nagy was born in 1896 in Transdanubia, in the Department of Somogy, of Calvinist parents. Calvinists constituted an insignificant minority in this part of the country, which was dominated by the Catholic Church. That may have been the reason, considered his biographer, that Nagy had acquired attitudes which were at times rebellious. It is not certain what the social position of his parents was, but they are believed to have been either modest landowners, artisans or rural merchants. It has also been suggested that there was some Jewish blood in the family, but this was never substantiated.

Nagy became acquainted with Communism in 1917, in revolutionary Russia, when he was twenty-one. As a man who grew up among Transdanubian peasants and who knew their problems well, he understood the spirit of the revolution. In this, he was different from other Hungarian Communists, most of whom came from petit-bourgeois backgrounds. Nagy understood the problems of servitude borne by the peasants, and their economic misery, as well as their innate dignity and their aspirations. Because of his acquaintance with the Hungarian peasants' hunger for land, he joined the Red Brigade, which was formed in Russia in 1918 and was composed of Austro-Hungarian prisoners-of-war. He returned to Hungary just after the Communist government of Bela Kun had been defeated. He then proceeded to organise agricultural workers into Communist organisations – a task made easier by the collapse of the Austro-Hungarian Empire and the chaos following the overthrow of the Communist regime. Perhaps because he was working in the countryside, not in the cities, he escaped the purges of Bela Kun's supporters, and was able to continue his party work.

However, in the following period he faced problems. His clandestine activities were finally noticed and he was given a three-year sentence by the Horthy regime. Following his release from prison in 1930 he came into conflict with the party's 'leftists'. During that time, the party, still under the leadership of Bela Kun, had the reputation of being the most sectarian and intrigue ridden of all the parties in the Communist International. It considered that its most dangerous enemies were the 'social fascists', in other words, the social democrats. Because of this, the emigré Hungarian Communists supported Stalin, rather than Bukharin. Nagy, on the other hand, expressed ideas which were in keeping with those of Bukharin, and he made statements to the effect that the party should abandon its isolation and acquire a following among the intellectuals and the peasants. Such views brought him into conflict with the policy of the Comintern; he was eventually forced to confess to his errors at a secret party congress, held in Moscow in early 1930. His self-criticism was later published in *Nepszabadsaq*.[10]

There can be no doubt that Nagy was a loyal Communist. The best proof of this was that, after his release from prison, he chose to go into exile in Moscow rather than stay on in Hungary. However, once in Moscow, he was forced to conform to the directives of the party leaders. The Moscow period shows Nagy exhibiting a certain duality in his attitudes: on the one hand, he wanted to conform to the party line out of loyalty to the leadership; on the other, he was prone to oppose certain party policies. Moreover, he tended to interpret Marxism–Leninism in a personal, puritan and humanitarian fashion; such an interpretation was bound to be harmful in the period of Stalinist purges. Following his humiliating encounter with the leadership, Nagy turned away from politics and began to study, taking a course at Moscow University. He then worked at the Soviet Institute of Agriculture. In 1937 he became the director of a *kolkhoz* in Siberia; it is uncertain whether he went there voluntarily, or whether it was a form of exile. However, from 1936 to 1940 he continued to contribute articles to the emigré journal, *Uj Hang*. His contributions dealt mainly with East European and Hungarian agrarian problems. In 1940 he was recalled to Moscow to meet the new leader, Rakosi, who had just arrived from Hungary. As has been mentioned above, Rakosi was then trying to reorganise the Hungarian party, which had been decimated and dispersed since the execution of Bela Kun.

As might have been expected, the tyrannical Rakosi and the phlegmatic farmer, whom some called a 'natural Christian', did not get on well together. Under the circumstances, they had to work together, but, in order to avoid clashing, they shunned each other. Nagy received a fairly minor post in the new organisation; he was appointed the editor of Radio Kossuth, the section of Radio Moscow which was being beamed to Hungary. The Hungarian section broadcast Hungarian classics, mainly the works of poets and writers from the period 1848–9. This choice of broadcasts suited Nagy's old-fashioned pronunciation of language, and possibly reflected his views much better than Stalinist propaganda. Finally, towards the end of the war in late 1944, Nagy joined the 'Muscovite' Communist convoy which was returning to Hungary with Rakosi at its head, transported by Red Army lorries. The newly arrived leaders had to make contact with home-based Communists such as Rajk, Kadar, Donath and others. Nagy was appointed minister of agriculture in the provisional government, which was set up in Debrecen (the capital of Hungarian Calvinism) on 23 December 1944.

In his new post, Nagy was responsible for carrying out the Hungarian land reforms. Though the reform was accomplished in great haste, and was presided over by the Soviet marshal, Voroshilov, it was considered a great success. The big estates were distributed among small peasants and farm labourers, and this resulted in Nagy acquiring many friends among non-Communist reformers. At the end of 1945, Nagy, who had become known in literary circles as 'Uncle Imre' because of his joviality, was appointed minister of the interior. However, in September 1947 this post was taken over by Laszlo Rajk, a veteran of the Spanish Civil War, and Nagy became the president of the National Assembly.

By 1948, Nagy's position in the Politburo had become precarious, because he opposed the hasty collectivisation measures demanded by the Kremlin. Like Rajk, but in a more cautious manner, he suggested a 'Hungarian way' to socialism. Rajk was more outspoken, and apparently even suggested at one point that he would mediate between Stalin and Tito in the Soviet–Yugoslav quarrel. It was this last transgression which ultimately led to Rajk's trial and execution. But both Nagy and Rajk were in danger when the big show trial of 'Titoists' was being prepared; and it has even been suggested that Beria and Rakosi hesitated whether to choose Rajk or Nagy as the main victim.[11]

The long series of purge trials in Eastern Europe in this period was so odious, and had such wide-ranging repercussions, that it is worth considering at this point whether the purges were in any way justified. It has been suggested that the Yugoslav split had heightened Stalin's persecution complex, and that, as a result, it was impossible to hold rational discussions in the CPSU leadership. An additional problem arose in connection with the United States' policy towards the Soviet Union and the Eastern Bloc. The American policy, aimed at isolating the socialist countries and at re-arming West Germany, alarmed the Soviet leadership. These two facts taken together explain, though they do not excuse, the purge trials. Another element was added by Beria's ambitions: keen to become the leader after Stalin's death, he profited by the panic created in satellite parties. Beria apparently wanted to amalgamate all the Communist parties into one centralised party, easier to keep under secret police supervision. This hypothesis is feasible, and Beria's speedy execution after Stalin's death seems to confirm at least part of it: that he had set his eyes on the highest post in the country. Thus, it may be true that Beria instituted the purges of foreign parties as a step towards attaining complete control over them, which would help him to attain his final aim. But even as Beria continued his attack on satellite parties, there were still some Communists who stood up to be counted. Nagy was among them.

Together with Joseph Revai, Nagy had voted in the Politburo against the execution of Rajk. This opposing vote put him in danger and isolated him from his colleagues. It was then recalled that in 1948 he had written a memorandum opposing hasty collectivisation; he was accused of being a Bukharinist. It was decided to expel him from the Politburo and to demand the usual recantation. The text of his statement was eventually published in *Nepszabadsaq* on 9 May 1957, but it is not certain whether it was published in full; it is thought that the text omitted passages in which Nagy made efforts to defend himself. Since the hasty collectivisation proved to be an economic catastrophe for Hungary, all those who had accused him of treason then, were later forced to apologise.[12]

These apologies had already been made in June 1953, when the Central Committee replaced Matyas Rakosi with Nagy as president of the Council of Ministers. Excuses were made for unjust treatment meted out to the new prime minister in the past, but owing to Rakosi's insistence, these apologies were never made public. In view of the rather shabby treatment which seemed to have been Nagy's fate each time he expressed doubts, one must ask why, yet again, he accepted his new post. Although he had escaped a trial in the last purge, he had experienced enough difficulty in the past to know what he could expect in the future. Furthermore, since the party had made so many mistakes, some of them fatal, why did he still believe that it should hold the monopoly of power? Some analysts insist that Nagy was a nebulous idealist, whose convictions made him lean towards a solution akin to Lenin's NEP (New Economic Policy), but who, nevertheless, believed firmly in central planning and state direction, though in a modified form. A simpler explanation might be that Nagy was simply swimming with the current, the only current he understood, and though at times his Calvinist conscience or his common sense made him protest against the worst excesses of the system, he was quite unable to abandon it.

Nagy's ambiguous attitudes were best seen during his period as prime minister, from 1953 to 1955, when he shared the leadership with Rakosi, which resulted in a duality of power. During all this time, the secretariat of the party, still led by Rakosi, attempted to neutralise all the initiatives of the prime minister. The contradictory directives issued from the two competing bodies made the country wonder who was in charge, and reduced confidence in the regime even further. There was constant tension between the state and the party apparatus, and this lasted until finally Rakosi took a long leave in the USSR in October 1954, in order to distance himself from the difficulties. However, his assistants continued to act as before, and questioned all of Nagy's decisions. Eventually, Nagy called a meeting of the Central Committee, and this body, uncertain of its powers because of Rakosi's absence, gave him a vote of confidence and accorded him full powers.

However, Rakosi had not been idle in the Soviet Union. He discovered that Nagy's policy was not in keeping with that of the new leaders, Khrushchev, Mikoyan and Bulganin, and was similar to the policy of the leader who had resigned, Malenkov. He then began to strive to remove Nagy from power. He was helped in this when, soon after Malenkov left his post at the beginning of 1955, Nagy had a heart attack which immobilised him for a few weeks. Rakosi used this period to deprive Nagy of office, though he seems to have overstepped his powers. It is believed that his mandate was simply to force Nagy to modify his policies, to conform with the new policies of the Soviet Union. When Nagy refused to do so, he was dismissed from his post and expelled from the Central Committee. Though Rakosi had gained his short-term aim of removing Nagy, the episode proved very harmful to him in the long run. Nagy resisted attempts to make him recant, and, since he had lost his official post, he became a legendary figure in the country. One commentator even believes that it was 'the legend of Nagy which undid Rakosi, more efficaciously than it would have been possible for a Nagy remaining . . . in the Central Committee'.[13]

Nagy may have become a legend in the country, but he lost none of his cautious, even hesitant, attitudes. After the conclusion of the Twentieth Congress of the CPSU in 1956, many of Nagy's friends suggested that he should set up an anti-Stalinist faction within the party. He refused to do so, and thus did not command as much support as he could have done. He was equally hesitant when the Hungarian revolution started, refusing to commit himself and declare which side he favoured. In the meantime, history was being made, almost as if in default. After several Soviet visits to Budapest, and many consultations, Mikoyan arrived in the city again on 29 October 1956. He conferred with the representatives of the Polish government and with some Hungarians. The Poles were in favour of appointing Nagy as leader, and, on behalf of the Soviet military, Marshal Zhukov also approved of the choice. A compromise was struck and on 30 October Radio Moscow made the official announcement that the working people of Hungary were behind Nagy and supported his programme. All might have proceeded as planned, had not the Revolutionary Committee of Defence, led by Maleter and Kiraly, decided to announce simultaneously that Hungary would leave the Warsaw Pact organisation and become a neutral state. For reasons which are difficult to understand even many years later, the ever-cautious and ever-loyal Nagy did not veto this announcement.[14] The sequel to the events is well known, and it is almost certain that Nagy signed his own death warrant when he acceded to Maleter's demands. What is not certain is why, for the first time in his political life, he went directly against Soviet orders. It is possible that the heady days of the Hungarian October gave him a new impetus for independence; or he may have felt strong enough to oppose Soviet orders for some other reason. It is also possible that he had no choice but to agree, because of pressures from the revolutionaries. When the revolution was quelled, Nagy sought asylum in the Yugoslav

Embassy; he was betrayed by the Yugoslavs, kidnapped and eventually executed. This epilogue will be touched upon later.[15]

Kadar after the catastrophe

Unlike Nagy, Kadar made the right choice. While he stood by Nagy in the early days of the revolution, on 4 November 1956, just as Soviet troops were entering Budapest, he announced that he had broken his links with Nagy and was setting up a rival, pro-Soviet government. The Hungarian game of musical chairs was over; Rakosi, Gero and Nagy were no longer there, and Janos Kadar, the quintessential pragmatist, had begun his long rule.

Compared with Nagy's varied and interesting career, that of Kadar is almost commonplace. However, there are some highlights in it, providing an insight into the history of the defunct Austro-Hungarian Empire, as much as into the workings of the Hungarian Communist Party. Kadar was born in 1912 in Fiume, on the Adriatic coast. (Fiume was then part of Austria–Hungary; it was renamed Rijeka when it became part of Yugoslavia after the Second World War.) Kadar's father abandoned his family and his mother settled in Budapest with her son. Young Janos Czermanik (his real name) became a machinist and joined the Hungarian Federation of Communist Workers in 1930. Since the Communist Party was illegal in Hungary at that time, he worked as a member of the Social Democratic Party. He was jailed twice for illegal activity; later on, from 1940 onwards, he helped to reconstruct the party and adopted the name of Kadar. He became a member of the Central Committee in 1942, and following the German occupation of Hungary, he was arrested while attempting to flee in April 1944 in order to reach Tito's headquarters in Yugoslavia.[16] After the defeat of the Germans, he became a member of the Greater Budapest Party Committee between 1945 and 1948; he was minister of internal affairs in 1948; and was arrested and imprisoned from 1951 to 1954. When he was released, he became party secretary for the Budapest district in 1954. He was made First Secretary of the Hungarian Socialist Workers' Party (the name the Communist Party adopted in 1948), and became prime minister after Nagy's removal in 1956.[17]

When he came to power in 1956, Kadar was perceived as a

bridge-builder and a conciliator, as well as a firm but cautious leader. This mode of leadership probably suited the country, still shaken by the revolution, and disoriented, first by Rakosi's terror, then by Nagy's 'Hamletism'. Some years later, a leading Hungarian intellectual expressed the country's mood in the following way:

> History has given us our share of suffering – the Turks, the Austrians and now the Russians. No one, not even the Russians, should blame us for trying to make something of our lives and our country. Call what we are doing socialist democracy, democratic socialism or just plain benevolent communism. What we need now . . . is some peace and quiet. We know we're being closely watched, and we are cautious. But we are moving ahead.[18]

In line with the above opinion, Kadar gave the country a pragmatic government, which was necessary at this stage. As has been seen, Kadar took the Soviet part during the revolution, but he never repudiated the revolution completely. His stated view was that it was intended to remedy the crimes of Rakosi and his accomplices; but the revolt had been exploited by counter-revolutionary forces, and the weakness of Nagy's government endangered the country's democratic system. Kadar also admitted that it was he who had asked the Soviet Union to intervene, in order that the forces of reaction might be crushed. Some commentators were surprised by Kadar's sudden change of camp; for, as late as 1 November, he had spoken on Budapest radio, extolling the revolution and announcing the reorganisation of the party. It has been pointed out that the key to Kadar's speech, however, lay in one sentence: he spoke of having to make a dramatic choice 'between the consolidation of our conquests and a move over to counter-revolution'. It almost seemed as though Kadar had taken over the mantle of loyalty to the CPSU which Nagy had borne for so long. Now that Nagy and his friends were ready to sacrifice the party, Kadar found the position unacceptable. It was noted that 'one may assume that Kadar, like Nagy, dreamed at first of reconciling devotion to the party and loyalty to the USSR with patriotism, and even with Hungarian nationalism, of whose strength he was well aware'. However, when a choice had to be made, he gave absolute priority to the interests of the party, rather than to those of national independence. Such an attitude demanded Soviet intervention, whatever the cost to the country.[19]

Of course, one may wonder whether other factors did not play a part in Kadar's decision. Personal ambition may have been one of those. In 1956, Kadar was still a relatively young man, but he had always been considered less able and less talented than Nagy. If Nagy was not removed, Kadar had little chance of gaining absolute power. The realisation of this may have made him inclined to seek Soviet intervention and consolidate his own position. If that was his aim, if ambition was his driving force, then he certainly succeeded.

However, to start with, Kadar faced stormy times. The popular anger at the brutal way in which the uprising was quelled was so great that Kadar was forced to make all the concessions on liberal reforms which Nagy had planned to carry out. His first period in power, therefore, was one of bowing to popular discontent. He conceded on all points, with the exception of one: he would not allow the creation of a multi-party system, or a secession from the Warsaw Treaty organisation. But in economic terms, Hungary was to be transformed into a post-Stalinist model of a socialist state, and it was hoped that the population would be mollified by this. When the economic measures did not succeed in toning down the national anger, Kadar resorted to the usual method: terror. He had the leader of the Workers' Council arrested (the Council was an independent organisation, modelled on the Petrograd Soviet), and gave Nagy and his companions, who had taken refuge in the Yugoslav Embassy, a safe pass to allow them to leave the country. It is not certain on whose orders – Kadar's or the Soviet military's – Nagy and the others were arrested on leaving the embassy, but they were then deported to Romania, where they were kept in confinement. They were eventually executed in June 1958, when a new wave of persecutions of 'Titoists' and 'revisionists' began. Again, it is not certain whether Kadar condoned Nagy's execution or not. It seems likely, however, that as Kadar began to enjoy power, he would see Nagy as a constant menace – a pretender who could come back to power, given favourable conditions. After all, power had changed hands so many times in Hungary, that another change would not be impossible. While Kadar may not have instigated Nagy's execution, such an outcome would have been welcome. It is not known what Kadar's reaction was to the execution of his old colleague, together with three other Communists. But there was a pleased reaction from the People's Republic of China, and in Europe, Prague, Sofia and Tirana were also gratified. On the other hand, there was distress in Poland and despair in Hungary. For all his professed liberalism, Kadar had lived up to the image of the bloodthirsty Rakosi. In 1958, Rakosi's ghost still hovered over the country.

Kadar's continuation in power owed much to his skilful diplomacy. Although he owed his initial successes to Nikita Khrushchev, he remained in power when Khrushchev was removed. Even though it has been said that he owed more to Khrushchev's patronage than any other East European leader, he outlasted him, as well as all the following Soviet leaders, until the election of Mikhail Gorbachev. His long period in power coincided with a period of modernisation of the Hungarian economic system. But it is doubtful if Kadar would have been able to restore the Hungarian economy so quickly after the revolution, had he not been able to call on Soviet aid, and had he not had the help of skilled economists, willing to develop new theories.

Kadar, however, must be given the credit for having agreed to carry out systemic reform; an act which many of the other leaders in the Bloc were afraid of. The foundations of the new policies were laid at the 1959 party congress, during which Kadar also managed to reinforce his own position. He carried out a purge in the party, during which he dismissed two ministers who might have been candidates for his post: Gyorgy Marosan, as well as the unpopular minister of agriculture, Imre Dogei, who had been responsible for collectivisation and who showed pro-Chinese tendencies. However, Kadar's main aim was to produce a climate of co-operation between the Communist government and all the classes in the country. This was difficult, as the intelligentsia had been particularly incensed by what it considered to have been Kadar's treacherous conduct – and it was to the intelligentsia that Kadar had to turn for help to create a more prosperous economy for the country. Thanks to massive Soviet aid and a reduction in military spending, it proved possible to raise the standard of living in the country. By 1960, the per capita income was 20 to 30 per cent higher compared to that of 1956.

Kadar did not neglect the decimated Hungarian party either; the number of members grew from 96,000 in 1956 to 512,000 in 1962 – though it was believed that most of the new members were either opportunists or pragmatists. As time passed, even the intellectuals began to accept Kadar's policy of compromise. It eventually dawned on them that the country had to become realistic in its attitudes toward the Soviet Union and that a totally negative attitude would be harmful for development. While the consensus was very fragile, it had been established. Moreover, Kadar promised more relaxation. In the early 1960s, Kadar published an article on Hungary – significantly enough published in the Moscow *Pravda* – in which he stated that 'despotism is not a socialist phenomenon'. He also launched a new slogan: 'He who is not against us, is with us'; a direct reversal of Lenin's early post-revolutionary slogan, which said that 'Who is not with us, is against us'.[20] The new liberalisation measures were aimed at elements hitherto thought to be hostile to the regime. For the first time since Stalinisation, wealthy peasants were to be admitted into co-operatives; educational discrimination against middle-class children was discontinued; and people who were not party members could be appointed to senior state and economic positions.

The last measure, in particular, met with strong opposition from party members, who had been accustomed to being appointed to senior posts for political reasons. However, Kadar and his advisers remained convinced that it was the right policy. In an article published in *Nepszabadsag* on 3 June 1962, he reaffirmed: 'The party is determined to arrive at a situation where senior positions in industry, agriculture, the civil service and culture are occupied by the most competent people.'[21] As a result of this strong stand, the relations between Communists and non-Communists improved gradually in 1962–3, and, in the end, it was the intelligentsia who profited most by the policies. Many of the writers who were given prison sentences after the uprising were released in the years 1960– 3. The party also improved its image by rehabilitating the victims of the Rakosi purges. In 1962, the Central Committee rehabilitated Rajk and other leaders who had been executed. Rakosi himself, Gero and seventeen other members responsible for the Stalinist measures were expelled from the party. Karoly Kiss, chairman of the party's Control Commission, was dismissed for opposing de-Stalinising measures.

Intellectual freedom began to be encouraged in this period. Censorship was relaxed, translations of Western works were published, and cinemas, theatres and journals were allowed to develop and publish as freely as possible under the circumstances. The

Hungarians were granted 'many freedoms, if not freedom itself', said an emigré writer. A Slovak journalist wrote that in Hungary 'freedom bears the name of socialism and Kadar is the most popular man in the country'.[22] Some steps were also taken to improve international relations. In the autumn of 1963, Kadar visited Belgrade and made up his quarrel with Tito, and in September of the same year, the Hungarian government reached an agreement with the Vatican on the appointments of bishops. However, the question of Cardinal Mindszenty, still sheltering in the American Embassy, was left unresolved.

Not all of Kadar's undertakings proved successful. In 1965, after visa requirements had been relaxed, there was a large exodus of technical intelligentsia. About four thousand doctors, engineers and technicians left the country, and the policy of granting visas had to be re-examined. At this stage, Kadar's closest associate, Istvan Szirmai, who was the countrys' leading ideologue, suggested ways of making Hungary more attractive by changing the political system. Several possibilities were discussed; among them, electoral reform, educational reform (which involved the abolition of screening prospective students for their class background for university admissions), and even embracing the Eurocommunist point of view, which rejected the Soviet Union's central place as a maker of ideological policies. From 1965 to 1968, the government was making efforts to pursue a campaign of cautious liberalisation of political institutions, to match the economic liberalisation. Unfortunately, the Czechoslovak crisis which occurred in 1968 almost obliterated all hopes of political reform.[23]

The Czechoslovak situation prompted fears in Hungary. 'Among most Hungarians, two sentiments seemed to predominate: on the one hand, the memories of 1956 were painfully revived; on the other, what almost amounted to a national psychosis developed out of fear for the security of the Hungarian reforms.' One strange aspect of this mass fear was the public concern about the fate of Janos Kadar, 'the one leader with whom the man-in-the-street associates the recent impetus towards the democratization of Hungarian life'.

Kadar himself, though he had become the torch-bearer of liberalisation in Eastern Europe, was appalled. Czechoslovakia had gone much further than Hungary; if he sided with the Czech reformers, his own position in Hungary could be threatened. On the other hand, if he opposed the Czechoslovak reforms, his own image as a liberaliser would be damaged. For, in the preceding period, Kadar's regime had become a model of liberalisation for all of Eastern Europe, though the picture was not of Kadar's own making. Therefore, the Czechs were told that they must stop their impetus toward reforms, 'and on no account overstep the bounds that the most liberal of the Communist leaders, Janos Kadar, had, in consultation with the Kremlin, set of liberalization in Hungary'.[24]

As always, Kadar behaved with a display of caution. Although it was publicly known that the invasion of Czechoslovakia had dismayed him, he did not proffer his views.

> For seven weeks following the invasion of Czechoslovakia, Kadar . . . went into self-imposed isolation. He was absent from all public functions, made no appearance of any kind and saw no one but his closest colleagues. Rumors of his fate, ranging from imprisonment in Moscow to suicide, swept Budapest.

A party member who knew Kadar well, noted that the situation was unusual: 'This is quite something, you know, to see apolitical people worrying over the man they despised only a year ago.' He then added: 'They called him Moscow's lackey then, and between that time and the execution of Imre Nagy in 1958 no Hungarian would have given you one forint for Kadar.' The changed climate was now reflected in the concern people felt for the leader: 'But look at them now. I heard two housewives talking, and when one said she had heard that Kadar had cut his own throat, the other deplored the possibility that there was no one to take his place. . . .'[25]

Kadar's low-profile act paid off; though it is doubtful if the Russians had really intended to force his resignation, in view of the fact that they were seriously panicking about the Czech crisis. At any rate, Kadar remained untouched; he eventually emerged from seclusion and laid to rest the fears for his own safety and that of the reforms. He assured the nation that he was still pursuing the reforms, and that he had the full approval of the Kremlin to do so. To the country's great relief, the government pursued the economic course, called the New Economic Mechanism. It is not known whether Kadar had any change of heart during those seven weeks of seclusion. It is doubtful if he was over-concerned for the Czech reformers, as he was himself instrumental in handing over his friends to the Russians in the past. Though reluctantly, he eventually endorsed the invasion of Czechoslovakia – again, no change of heart there. The most likely explanation seems to be that he eluded the public in order not to be forced to make any statements on the Czechoslovak situation – a position which must have been noticed by shrewd observers. Nevertheless, it is a measure of his changed standing in the country that the man who had been called 'Moscow's lackey' had suddenly become the country's beloved leader.

The fact that Kadar was suddenly perceived as the country's saviour may have had more to do with the changed attitudes of the Hungarians, than with the changed attitudes of Kadar himself. The traumatic experience of the revolution must have matured the nation enough to give it a clearer perception of Hungary's geopolitical situation. Hungary had been alone in 1956, and it was still alone in 1968, while a powerful patron and neighbour watched over it. No one wanted any more revolutions and sacrifices. Kadar and his team were also seen to have delivered at least some of the goods needed by the people, and to have provided a modicum of liberalisation. 'Some freedoms' were allowed, and this made the nation feel that any changes in the leadership would be a change for the worse. In addition, Kadar had gradually acquired the status of a statesman, and the Hungarians began to feel that their country was beginning to count in the international scene because of this.

Kadar, the statesman and the consequences

It is difficult to analyse how and why Kadar became a statesman, and began to be admired both in the Socialist Bloc and in the West. But on the face of it, it would seem that the same factors which motivated the Hungarians to become more realistic played a role in his changed status. Gradually, Kadar moved from his previous position of total loyalty to the CPSU, and was ready to try out new ideas and even, at times, to challenge the Soviet Union. Part of the reason for this change may have been his choice of advisers. After the death of his chief adviser, Istvan Szirmai, he chose Gyorgy Aczel to be his closest associate. Aczel had been a Stalinist who had undergone a complete conversion. He became one of Kadar's closest friends, while, at the same time, remaining on good terms with non-Communist literary dissenters. It was owing to his advice that Kadar made history in May 1969, when he paid an unprecedented visit to Eotvos Lorand University in Budapest, in order to introduce the New Economic Mechanism. He stood in his shirtsleeves before a packed auditorium, explained for some five hours the problems of the nation and later answered questions freely and with candour. Another sensation was created by Aczel the following month, when he made an address to the party's Political Academy, the highest educational body of the party. He set out a programme of reorganisation of sciences, which introduced new and bold concepts. The scientists who discussed the programme perceived a new, humanistic approach which, they felt, could also have consequences in the field of liberal arts. Aczel's theory was based on a return to research-based universities, rather than, as was the case at that time, concentrating research in institutes which were under the control of the Academy of Sciences. At the same time, Aczel also rehabilitated the social science of sociology, which had been condemned during the Stalinist period, and he reaffirmed the concept of trial and error in research.

More startling events were due. On the anniversary of Laslo Rajk's sixtieth birthday, a Budapest street was named after him by the city authorities. At the same time, an article in a literary journal questioned the reasons for Rajk's trial and execution. In June, the same journal carried a response from Rajk's widow, who had been silent for many years, calling for an investigation of the case. When the new pro-Rajk campaign began, there was some excitement in the country, for it was common knowledge that at the time of his arrest, the minister of the interior had been Janos Kadar, who was also one of Rajk's closest friends.

> Thus a number of intellectuals expressed the opinion . . . that the articles were opening up a Pandora's Box which might have far-reaching repercussions, since it was generally believed that Rajk had 'confessed' at the urging of Kadar, who in turn had been ordered by Rakosi to convince Rajk that his admission of guilt was for the good of the party.[26]

Despite this, Kadar does not seem to have suffered as a result of the campaign, though it is puzzling that the campaign should have been started at this particular time. It has been suggested that

Kadar wanted to have the issue of Rajk's execution aired at this stage, before he began to open Hungary to influences from outside the Bloc, in order to demonstrate how cruel and bloodthirsty Rakosi had been, and how he had been pressed to deliver his best friend to the executioner. On the other hand, it may well be that Kadar, by then accepted both by the CPSU and the Hungarians as the best man to lead the country, felt secure enough to have the Rajk affair cleared out of the way.

Gyorgy Lukas, the Marxist philosopher, summed up the feelings of the people, when he said that after the Czechoslovak reform movement had been liquidated, Kadar had done the right thing:

> Kadar is probably the best man we could have had for what had to be done. And what had to be done is still going on. . . . But if there is a step backward here and there . . . it is a mistake to hold this against Kadar or anyone around him. Some of those people know what Stalinism is, and none better than Kadar, who was imprisoned by Rakosi, tortured and humiliated. . . . Kadar will never return Hungary to the pre-1956 era.[27]

At the time of these events, Kadar was still a relatively young man, apparently in good health. He did not experience much opposition either from within or from outside the party. Because of these factors, he was able to experiment and to liberalise, without losing any of his power. His ability to lead the country was admired by other leaders, and this was demonstrated in the way he was treated by them. The Tenth Congress of the party, held in November 1970, was attended by thirty-one delegations from sister parties, and the CPSU delegation was led by Leonid Brezhnev himself. Other foreign delegations were also led by their first secretaries. Moreover, the party itself was much stronger. In 1970, the number of party members was 662,397. By the time the Eleventh Congress was about to be held, the numbers rose to 742,397 members; that is, an increase of 80,000. A commentator noted that part of the party's popularity was due to Kadar's policy of retaining the same people in their positions for as long as possible. 'Stability of personnel seems to have always been one of the principles of the Kadar regime's policy, in sharp constrast to the frequent zigzags that had occurred during the Rakosi era.'

Kadar took care to see that, though long-serving, his advisers were relatively youthful. In 1975, the average age of the Hungarian

Politburo was 59.05 years (which was young in terms of other Bloc countries), but despite this, none of the members was inexperienced. All but one of them had joined the party between 1931 and 1945, and it was noted that 'this means that the present Politburo in its totality stems from an epoch of party history – the prewar and World War II underground periods – whose exploits are increasingly fading from the memory of the younger generation of party members'.[28]

Although there were those who thought that Kadar ought to have resigned at this stage, this would have been difficult to put into operation: 'Kadar's personality . . . plays such a pivotal role in Hungary, as the main guarantee against unwelcome changes, that it is quite unlikely that either the Hungarian party or the CPSU would be willing to let him retire at a time of serious economic strain and stress.' While acquiring the reputation of being ready to subordinate his personal interests to those of the party, it seemed too that Kadar was not ready to leave office. A discreet cult of personality had been built up around him – whether by design or by chance –and this was expressed by the First Secretary of the Municipal Party Committee in Budapest, who wished Kadar many more years in office, hoping that 'he long continue, in good health, his responsible work for the benefit of the Hungarian people and the international workers' movement'.[29]

However, though liberal in Hungary, Kadar displayed less liberal views in relation to non-conformists abroad. He was strongly opposed to Eurocommunism and maintained that the Soviet party must play a leading role in the shaping of the international Communist movement. However, this was not an ideological stand; though he was a skilful player, Kadar had never emerged as a member of either camp; he was not a conservative Communist, but neither was he a liberaliser. One must come to the conclusion that most of his life was spent in finding pragmatic solutions for the problems of his party and the country. This could be the reason that he outlasted most of the other East European leaders: he proved to be a better problem-solver than most.

Inevitably, his rule had to come to an end. In May 1988, when Kadar was approaching his seventy-sixth birthday and had been in power for thirty-one years, a party conference made strong criticisms of his management. Views about the state of the economy and the party were particularly strident. 'A senior party official . . .

refused . . . to confirm widespread reports that Mr Kadar would be replaced on Sunday by Prime Minister Karoly Grosz,' commented a correspondent.[30] As a matter of fact, Kadar was outvoted on 22 May, and was replaced by Grosz. It is known that Kadar did not want to give up power, but was forced to do so, both because of his age, and because of pressure by the Gorbachev leadership to put younger men in charge.

However, Kadar did not forget the power that had made him. Interviewed a few months later, he said that he had no regrets about any of his actions, including the request for Soviet troops to intervene in 1956. He affirmed that 'the system did give something to the people, and some of them feel endangered now. . . . The political system of capitalist society . . . cannot be restored. However much is being denied, those who received a lot from the system would not tolerate that.'[31]

Karoly Grosz, who succeeded Kadar in 1988, is a man of Gorbachev's generation. Fifty-seven years old, he has been a party *apparatchik* since his youth. Because of his relative youth, he has never been in the underground movement, never been to prison, and never been tortured. If he had betrayed his closest friends (which is not impossible), they would not have been hanged. He is the new type of Communist leader: interested in efficiency, order and prosperity. But he had never been a liberal and made it plain at the outset that he would not follow the advice of those who wished to liberalise further. It so happened that he had to modify his stance a year later, as will be seen in the concluding chapter. But he did not set out to become the torch-bearer of liberalisation. Rather, like Mikhail Gorbachev, he wanted to improve productivity and to modernise the country's industrial base, as well as to further scientific research.[32] It is too early to say whether he will be successful in this aim. But even if he is, it is doubtful if he can ever become a symbol of national pride and independence, like Nagy, or of national regeneration, like Kadar. In Hungary, as in the rest of Eastern Europe, the time for heroism has passed. The era of realism has been embraced with both hands. This may be very good for the econony, but it does spell the death of ideology. And some observers may think that Communism without its ideological base has no future.

Notes

1. B. Kovrig, *Communism in Hungary from Kun to Kadar*, p. 132.
2. *Ibid.*, pp. 132–3.
3. Harry G. Shaffer, 'Progress in Hungary', *Problems of Communism*, January–February 1970.
4. Kovrig, *Communism*, pp. 156–7.
5. Fejto, *A History*, p. 112.
6. Kovrig, *Communism*, pp. 244–5.
7. *Ibid.* p. 245.
8. Fejto, *A History*, p. 113. However, Kovrig provides different dates and a slightly different account. See *Communism*, pp. 268–9.
9. Fejto, *Portrait d'Imre Nagy: un communiste qui a choisi le peuple*; an introduction to Nagy's work, entitled *Un Communisme qui n'oublie pas l'homme*, p. 5.
10. Published on 9 May 1957. For a full account of the conflict, see Fejto, *Portrait*, pp. 7–8.
11. Fejto, *Portrait*, pp. 9–13.
12. *Ibid.*, pp. 14–15.
13. *Ibid.*, p. 27.
14. *Ibid.*, pp. 43–4.
15. For a brief account of the Hungarian Revolution, see Narkiewicz, *Marxism*, pp. 184–5.
16. Kovrig, *Communism*, pp. 138 and 144.
17. *Who's Who in Socialist Countries*.
18. E. Sandor, 'Hope and caution', *Problems of Communism*, January–February 1970.
19. Fejto, *A History*, p. 122.
20. *Pravda*, 26 December 1961; also see Fejto, *A History*, p. 167.
21. Quoted by Fejto, *A History*, p. 168.
22. *Kulturny Zivot*, No. 16, 1961, quoted by Fejto, *A History*, p. 169.
23. Sandor, *Hope*.
24. *Ibid.*, and Fejto, *A History*, p. 223.
25. Sandor, *Hope*. Statement attributed to an unnamed Hungarian Communist.
26. Sandor, *Hope*.
27. Lukacs, quoted by Sandor, *Hope*.
28. RFE *Situation Report*, 11 March 1975.
29. *Ibid.*
30. 'Delegates assail Kadar as party session opens', *International Herald Tribune*, 21 May 1988, and 'Hungarian Communists replace Kadar as chief of party, Grosz elevated', *International Herald Tribune*, 23 May 1988.
31. *The Eternal Conviction of Janos Kadar*, interview with Flora Lewis, *International Herald Tribune*, 10 October 1988.
32. 'Un homme d'appareil accepté par les réformistes', *Le Monde*, 24 May 1988. The article also contained a brief biography of Karoly Grosz.

6

From Gomulka to Jaruzelski

A patriotic Communist

The Soviet Union has probably experienced more problems in Poland than in any other country of the Bloc. It is probable that, had Poland not been needed so badly to keep the route to East Germany open, the Russians might have opted to move out of the country, leave the Poles to their own fate, and forget the socialist experiment. The key to Soviet problems lay in several centuries of turbulent history, rather than in the opposition to the Soviet brand of Marxism; but it was the latter which was stressed much more strongly. The Polish–Russian relationship in mid-twentieth century was not a very happy one, and it only followed the pattern of several centuries of strife, wars, treachery and aggression. The Polish victory in the Soviet–Polish war, soon after the setting up of the socialist state, and the annexation of half of Poland in 1939, thanks to the Nazi–Soviet Pact, completed the history of bad neighbourly relations. Well before Marxism and the Soviet Union was conceived, the two countries had a history of adversarial relations which kept them in a state of cold war – often to turn to a hot war at a moment's notice.

The long-lived traditional enmity was accentuated during the Stalinist period, because the Poles felt they were the most oppressed nation in the Bloc and that they suffered both economically and politically. Hence, there was much jubilation in Poland when the 'Thaw' occurred and a new, non-Stalinist, native leader,

Wladyslaw Gomulka, was carried shoulder-high by the Warsaw crowd on his installation as the new head of the party. Gomulka was a new type of Communist leader, whose life history is well worth recounting in brief.

In a way, Gomulka was as much a 'survivor' as Honecker. He had been born in Krosno, then part of the Austro-Hungarian Empire, in 1905. Krosno was situated in the oil-bearing region of what was then known as Galicia, one of the few industrialised areas in a highly agricultural region. Because of the political reforms forced on the Austro-Hungarian government, Galicia was also the one part of former Poland which enjoyed self-government. There were free political parties and autonomous educational and cultural institutions. It was, therefore, natural for a young Galician to be a Polish patriot, because he had been brought up in the Polish cultural traditions which had to be preserved for future generations.

Another special feature of Galicia was its strong Socialist Party which formed part of the large Austrian Socialist Party. Gomulka's father was a socialist trade unionist; he himself became a trade union organiser at the age of sixteen. He had been apprenticed to a blacksmith, though he does not appear to have completed his apprenticeship. His Communist activity began in the 1920s when he worked for the Union of Chemical Workers in the oil industry in his home territory – south-eastern Poland. In 1932, after the Communist Party had been declared illegal, he was arrested and sentenced to four years in prison. However, he was soon released on health grounds and went back to underground work. He was arrested again in 1936 and sentenced to seven years' imprisonment. This time he was not released until the outbreak of the Second World War in September 1939. He publicly disapproved of the Soviet–Nazi Pact of August 1939, and later urged the Comintern to organise a Communist underground to fight the Nazis. He himself fought against the Germans in the defence of Warsaw in September 1939. In this matter, he was completely at variance with the official Stalinist policy, which claimed that the war was an imperialist one and did not concern the Communists.

Gomulka's firm convictions were rewarded after the outbreak of the Soviet–Nazi war. He became the secretary of the Warsaw branch of the PPR (the initials of the Polish Workers' Party – the name, at this time, of the Polish Communist Party) in December

1942, and, at the end of the war, he became a member of the party's Central Committee. He was elected general secretary of the PPR in November 1943, at a time when relations between the Polish party and the CPSU were particularly acrimonious. While his rapid promotion may have been due to his leadership qualities, a more likely reason was probably the speed with which the Communists were being eliminated by the Nazis.

It must not be forgotten that, under Nazi occupation, the posts of responsibility in the party were not sinecures. Pawel Finder, the general secretary of the PPR prior to Gomulka, and Malgorzata Fornalska, a member of the Central Committee, were captured by the Gestapo in the autumn of 1943, and never reappeared alive. The previous general secretary, Marceli Nowotko, was assassinated in Warsaw in November 1942 in mysterious circumstances. During the liquidation of the uprising in the Warsaw Ghetto, 'The Gestapo seized the PPR's chief press organ, "Liberty Tribune", and arrested many leading party members. To some extent these arrests might have reflected the struggle for power which went on among the leadership of the PPR', commented one writer.[1]

There have been many rumours about Communists informing on each other in the German Communist Party after Hitler came to power, as well as in the French Communist Party during the Second World War. It is difficult to establish how much truth there was in such rumours. But it must be stressed that, if the same were true of the Polish party, such behaviour would appear even more bizarre. The Nazi occupation of Poland was so brutal as to make it difficult even to organise a minimum of resistance, and even more difficult to stay out of the Gestapo's hands. The top posts in the party were not desirable jobs, but were the best means towards arrest, torture and death. It is possible that there were some infiltrators who denounced the Communists to the Gestapo; it is also probable that under physical pressure, some members were named, but by and large the Communist Party, like the rest of the nation, had proved that it was faithful to its ideals and opposed to Nazism. In view of this, it is not credible to suggest that the top leaders informed on each other in order to succeed to better posts.

Owing to the confused situation and lack of records, it is impossible to establish with any certainty that Gomulka was a participant in any party struggle, or, indeed, whether there was any struggle. However, due to the death of the two previous secretaries at the hands of the Gestapo, he did become general secretary, remained in his post until the German troops retreated from Poland, and managed to stay alive during this period. This, in itself, was something of a record. After the liberation of the country, he became one of the main Communist leaders – people who tried to construct a new socialist Poland, a new democracy. Gomulka is on record as saying that this new democracy would be sponsored by 'the working class, led by the Marxist–Leninist parties'. His convictions were strengthened by the wartime experience, and he was intent on establishing socialism in the country because as he put it 'our party . . . has been tempered by the hard struggle against the German occupation, our blood and our lives are the foundation stone of the reborn Poland. We pioneered her liberation. Blood and combat have given us the right to determine her future and character.'

Despite his apparent willingness to compromise with the rest of the nation (which, as he well knew, was both anti-Soviet and anti-Russian), Gomulka displayed a ruthless side to his character when he was negotiating with the Polish emigré government in London. While he was holding talks in Moscow with Stanislaw Mikolajczyk, who represented the London emigré government, Gomulka stated plainly that his party was not prepared to share power with anyone:

> Please take no offence . . . that we offer you only such governmental posts as we consider expendable. It is because it is we who are in power. . . . We will never surrender the power we have seized. . . . If a government of national unity cannot be established, perhaps several hundred people will be killed but this will not frighten us. . . . We will ruthlessly destroy all reactionary bandits.[2]

The 'bandits' to whom Gomulka referred were the underground Home Army, a legitimate government organisation, but one opposed to a compromise with the Communists. It can be seen from this that, unlike the Italian and the French parties, which were in alliance with the non-Communist parties when in the underground, the Polish party refused to concede any power, and this was matched by the refusal of the non-Communist bodies to come to any agreement with the Communists. In the context of the historical precedents and the underlying complex issues, this was, perhaps, not surprising, but the outcome proved to be tragic for the future of Poland within the Socialist Bloc. In some ways it was perhaps fitting that, having helped to establish a socialist government, Gomulka himself was accused of anti-socialist activity.

It can be seen from the above that in Poland a different situation prevailed from that of the other Bloc countries, where internal party struggles gave an added impetus to intra-party persecution. In Poland the question turned much more round a struggle between two opposing trends within the party: the 'nationalist' one, as personified by Gomulka, and the 'internationalist' one, which was equated with the Stalinist wing of the party. When Stalin developed the policy of integrating Eastern Europe and began to put it into operation, Gomulka became a liability to the Soviet Union. The Cold War was in its initial stages. Gomulka's doubts about Soviet guarantees on Poland's new Western frontier, coupled with his insistence on the 'Polish way to socialism', created an impression in Moscow that he was not as reliable as had been thought. Gomulka himself made matters worse in June 1948. Just as the Cominform was about to condemn Tito for his 'nationalist deviation', Gomulka made a speech praising the independence of the Polish Socialist Party, a long-time foe of the Communists.

He was made to pay dearly for his outspokenness. At a Central Committee meeting which took place from 31 August until 3 September 1948, he was criticised by all those present. His attempts to compromise between the Stalinist course and the 'Polish road to socialism' were denounced. He was accused of being a 'nationalist deviationist' who wanted to negotiate with the CPSU as an equal, and of being thirsty for power. He resigned during the meeting and his resignation was accepted with alacrity. Eye-witnesses testified that Gomulka broke down after beginning his first sentence of self-criticism, which ran as follows: 'Comrades, I have erred . . .', and the rest of the recantation had to be read by Bierut, while the weeping Gomulka sat at a nearby table.[3]

It is quite possible that Gomulka's repentance and breast-beating saved him from the fate of the other leaders in the Bloc. It is not known whether he had been advised to behave in this manner by his successor, who had no wish for a blood-bath, or whether his own sense of self-preservation dictated this behaviour. At any rate, his life was saved, and he was merely placed under arrest for several years. He remained a member of the party for one more year after the passage of these dramatic events, but was eventually expelled in November 1949, and placed under house arrest in July 1951. For two years his trial was awaited, but in vain. Despite Soviet pressure, no trial was arranged, even though the 'Muscovite' wing of the party had gained a victory over the 'natives'. One of the reasons for this untypical behaviour may have been the fact that the 'natives' were mostly ethnic Poles, whereas the 'Muscovites' were, in the main, non-ethnics. Another reason may have been Gomulka's high standing in the country, a fact the 'Muscovites' could not ignore. Whatever the reason, Gomulka lived to see the death of Stalin and the return to a semblance of normality within the Bloc. In that he was more fortunate than most of the other leaders, with the possible exception of Tito and Kadar.

It has been suggested by some analysts that Gomulka's fall may have been due more to his sudden rise to power than to his latent Titoism. 'It seems quite probable . . . that Gomulka's spectacular rise to power turned his head. He became jealous of Soviet interference and resentful of the colonial methods of exploitation applied in Poland by the Kremlin.' Before his fall, Gomulka was the general secretary of the party and a deputy prime minister. Though he had to share power with Bierut and Berman, it is possible that these two positions may have given him too much confidence in his own powers, particularly in view of his modest origins and his lack of experience in government. Alternatively, it has been thought that he was traditionally inclined towards the patriotic form of socialism, connected with the PPS (the Polish Socialist Party), a socialism that has been described as 'militant and spontaneous, romantic and emotionally patriotic'. He often disparaged the Luxemburgist heritage in the Polish Communist Party because of its anti-nationalist stance and its disregard of agricultural problems. It is thought that he wanted a genuine synthesis of both movements, the socialist and the Communist, which would have balanced the party and given it some standing in the country. In view of the social and political developments in the country since that period, there must be many people in both the Polish party and the CPSU who regret that Gomulka was not allowed to put his theories into practice. Such a development might have saved many problems.

But while Gomulka was still attempting to effect a quick merger of the socialist and Communist parties and was searching for a 'Polish road to socialism', the Soviet leadership, together with the

'Muscovites' in the PPR, decided that he had the making of another Tito. 'Here, it seems, lay the main cause of Gomulka's downfall: he was not Bolshevized enough or Stalinized enough, not indoctrinated deeply enough to accept the leadership of the Soviet Union, that is, complete and automatic subservence of his party and his country to the Bolshevik party and the Soviet state,' concluded one writer.[4]

It must be stressed here that the picture outlined above is in complete contrast to the picture of Gomulka in Moscow, dictating terms of surrender to the ministers of the emigré government. But it need not be necessarily faulty. It may have seemed easy enough in Moscow to exclude all the non-Communists from a future Polish government; but a few years of governing in post-war Poland may have instilled a more realistic attitude in him. Gomulka probably concluded that governing without the consensus of the nation was producing disastrous results. If the country decided to resist Communist rule, even a reign of terror by the secret police would prove unsuccessful. Therefore it was in the best interests of the party, as well as of the Soviet Union, to come to some understanding with the opposition, in order to improve relations between the opposing forces. But unfortunately, as soon as Gomulka came to those conclusions, he was removed from office. Naturally, there was no guarantee that he would have been successful had he stayed in office. Though a loyal Communist and apparently a patriot, he was not trained in administration and his experience of government was negligible. He had spent most of his youth in underground trade union activity or in prison. Wartime found him in underground resistance; a marginal resistance movement, which did not co-operate with the legitimate Home Army. He had spent the early post-war years in trying to eliminate opposition to Communist government. In addition, Gomulka had had a very limited education and tended to become autocratic when uncertain of his arguments. All these factors proved to be his undoing in the late 1940s; and they were to prove even more harmful when he was finally called back to govern the country in 1956, after he had spent several years under house arrest. The task he was entrusted with then demanded a great deal of flexibility and talent; he was expected to re-structure the country in an image which was socialist but non-Stalinist.

The need for re-structuring in 1956 was urgent, because the

Poznan riots in June gave the party a tremendous shock. After twelve years in power, the party suddenly had to face the fact that it did not carry much weight either with the industrial workers, or with the young generation. In the wake of the riots, the Seventh Plenum of the Central Committee, which convened for an unprecedented ten-day period, began on 18 July 1956. The Plenum rehabilitated Gomulka and his associates, Spychalski and Kliszko. Three new members of the Politburo were elected: Edward Gierek, Roman Nowak and Adam Rapacki; and it is notable that all three had had experience of working or living in Western Europe. However, despite the apparent new democratic trends, the whole future leadership of the country for the next two decades was decided by one plenary meeting of the Central Committee – a fact which may have had something to do with future events.

Gomulka's return to power was hailed as a great victory; in the previous period he had become a symbol of resistance to Soviet pressures, like Imre Nagy in Hungary. Though he was a hero to the party rank-and-file, 'to many non-Communists, this man, who had been the personification of Soviet occupation between 1945 and 1948, became the epic warrior who had challenged Stalin and his stooges, who had fought for some independence from Moscow, and who had suffered imprisonment because of his courageous stand'. In other words, he had become a martyr for the Polish cause, and was forgiven his Communism and his past because of this.

Unfortunately, the man who came back from the wilderness in 1956 was not much changed from the man who had been eliminated in the early 1950s. This may explain why a leader who was carried to power on the shoulders of the people in October 1956, became the scapegoat of the same people a decade and half later. Most of the blame was attached to his inability to carry out his earlier promises. When he was elected First Secretary on 21 October, Gomulka outlined a future plan of action in which he promised to eliminate corruption, waste and oppression, and vowed to raise the standard of living. The conclusions of the Eighth Plenum were greeted with genuine enthusiasm, because the people, having accomplished one 'miracle' – the return of Gomulka to power – were now waiting for another one: that of a better and more comfortable life.

It turned out, however, that Gomulka was not a miracle-maker, and that he had made the mistake of promising too much. The mistake on the part of the people was that they placed too much confidence in his capacity to govern. One analyst concluded that the secret of the success of the October 1956 revolution was that the party had a reserve team of popular leaders, who were the victims of Stalin's 'personality cult', and that it restored them to power without causing a civil war.[5] While this opinion is apt, it does not take into account the conditions of the period. The reality was that the country was politically and economically bankrupt; that it was bereft of trained officials to run the machinery of the state; and that the new leaders' governing abilities were almost completely untested. The only experience the new team had acquired was in undergrond work during the war, and a few years governing a Stalinist state. They were now expected to run a socialist democratic state, which had, in the meantime, been severely destabilised. It is doubtful if any of the new leaders understood what the term represented, and it is certain that objective conditions for introducing such a government in Poland simply did not exist.

In view of the above, it is hardly surprising that Gomulka became disillusioned within a short period of time, and that his name lost glamour both within party circles and in the country. He soon became the butt of popular jokes; in the people's eyes he became an elderly, inflexible autocrat, given to telling anecdotes, but showing little interest in the nitty-gritty of government. As the situation in the country went from bad to worse, propelled only by its own impetus, the nation was eager for a change. Yet it took another uprising to remove Gomulka from power.

A technocratic Communist

When writing about the Gomulka government in the late 1960s, one writer noted that he had used his authority as a prominent victim of Stalinist repression 'to manipulate and dominate opposed factional groupings in the supreme leadership of the Polish United Workers' party'. In keeping with the Polish tradition, there were several factions within the party. In the first place, there were the former socialists; another group comprised the technocrats, headed by the first secretary of Silesia, Edward Gierek, and the group which was nicknamed the 'Jewish liberal' group, a self-explanatory term. Other groups, not quite so important, were also known to exist. Gomulka steered between all these factions: 'The enforced cooperation of disparate groupings was consonant with Gomulka's personal penchant for policies which, while avoiding any consistent effort to suppress intellectual dissent or engage in a more vigorous struggle with the Church . . . have precluded any serious consideration of liberal proposals toward modernizing Polish society.'[6]

This opinion confirms one's worst suspicions about Gomulka's methods of government. He had been given a chance to improve the nation's political and economic situation, and, after a few significant but insufficient moves towards liberalisation, he wasted the opportunity completely. Instead of reforming the corrupt bureaucracy and improving the efficiency of state-run enterprises, he spent his time on intrigues and the occasional soothing of his associates. He ignored the greatest power in the country, the Catholic Church, trying not to attack it but, on the other hand, not making any important concessions. Since he came to power almost by chance, he used almost all of his energy in trying to retain that power. But perhaps little more could have been expected of a personality the calibre of Gomulka. Nevertheless, his period in office did produce some positive developments.

The persecution of the regime's opponents was stopped, and a measure of free expression was allowed to the intellectuals. Both measures would have been unthinkable in the Stalinist period. However, towards the end of his period in power, Gomulka spoiled his record by condemning the 'cosmopolitan elements' and blaming them for the problems the country was facing. Though one is inclined to make allowances because of the manifold difficulties he was facing, it must be spelled out that – behind all the façade of liberalism and good will – Gomulka had no discernible policy of any kind. He remained what he had always been: a former trade union organiser, struggling with a post which was too big for him. It was this lack of policy which led to Gomulka's final downfall.

Some time before he was removed, it had been suggested that a new leadership stratum would soon emerge – one which was better qualified to govern – and that the 'Gomulka era' would soon be over. A new era, dominated by a rationalising and modernising 'national Communist' élite, was about to begin. This suggestion, voiced in 1969, was to prove correct.

Gomulka came to power in the wake of a workers' uprising. He was removed from power during another period of rioting. This time, the venue was changed. The riots began in the Baltic city of Gdansk. As the workers in the city demonstrated against an increase in the prices of food and fuel made just before Christmas 1970, it was announced on 19 December that Gomulka had been replaced as first secretary by Edward Gierek. Gierek, 'the unofficial "crown prince" since the Fourth Congress in 1964, was the obvious successor when the PZPR [Polish United Workers' Party, also known as PUWP] central *aktyw* and the Soviet leadership . . . decided that they had no stomach for another Krondstadt'.[7]

It was noted at that time that 'Gierek himself is symbolic of . . . change. His whole background differs strikingly from that of the predominantly intellectual-ideologue types who ran the party under Gomulka.'[8] Gierek was born in 1913 in a mining community near Bedzin. His father was a miner who is believed to have died in a mining accident when Edward was a child. Edward emigrated to France in 1923 (presumably with his family), and began work as a miner at the age of thirteen. He was expelled from France in 1934, and it is known that he arrived in Belgium in 1937. None of his official biographies mentions the period from 1934 to 1937; therefore it is concluded that he either lived illegally in one of those two countries, or that he was away on some unspecified business. It is possible that he was in Moscow or that he worked as a Comintern agent, as so many Communists did at that time. In this period, he married and had two sons. When war broke out and after the German occupation of Belgium, he became one of the organisers of the Belgian resistance movement. Following the end of the Second World War he became the chairman of the National Council of Poles in Belgium. He was also the organiser of the Polish Workers' Party and of the Union of Polish Patriots in Belgium from 1945 to 1948. He returned to Poland in 1948 and started to work in the Polish mining region of Silesia.

Gierek became the secretary of the PUWP for the Katowice region of Silesia in 1949. At the same time, he began university studies graduating as a mining engineer from an extra-mural course at the Krakow Academy of Mining and Metallurgy in 1954, when he became head of the party's Heavy Industries Department at the Central Committee. In 1956, he was elected to the Politburo and appointed secretary of the Central Committee, becoming first secretary of the party in the Katowice region in 1957.[9]

During the period when he was in charge of the coal mining industry, Gierek became famous for his administrative skills; he had also managed to acquire an academic background suitable for his new post, albeit rather late in life. Perhaps the most unusual factor about Gierek's career is that he was the first Polish Communist leader to have lived abroad for a long time, both before and after the Second World War, and that he had remained loyal to the party throughout this period. His return to Poland, to conditions which were extremely difficult, may have had a bearing on his rapid promotion in his native country. Altogether, his career was as different from that of Gomulka as could possibly be imagined. But it was not a career without some drama. His accession to the top post was not a foregone conclusion, though he rose steadily in party ranks. Had it not been for the fact that good administrators were desperately needed at the end of the Gomulka period, he may have been passed over for someone with whom the Politburo felt more at ease.

When he was appointed First Secretary of the PUWP, Gierek was already fifty-seven years old. He had spent almost ten years and a lot of energy in the reconstruction of the Silesian mining industry and had made Silesia the show-piece of Polish economy. Although he used to come to Warsaw for meetings and conferences, Silesia was his base and it was the area he understood best. This proved a major problem when he came to Warsaw for a permanent post. The main reason for this was that he tended to treat the capital as though it was Katowice on a bigger scale; he could not understand that the two cities were completely different in almost every respect. Even the language of the inhabitants of the two differs in many respects and the mentality is entirely dissimilar. Gierek also alienated many people in the leadership by introducing too many of his Silesian mining friends into the Politburo and the Central Committee. Several of the new appointees had a similar background to his own; they had worked and lived in France and Belgium. 'The different background of the new ruling élite undoubtedly accounts for the fact that their social philosophy and political styles also differ radically in many respects from those of the Gomulka group,' commented one analyst.

Gierek's colleagues were not professional revolutionaries, but administrators. They tended to be less inclined towards ideology, and were more interested in pragmatic solutions, unlike their predecessors. While they were all loyal Communists, nurtured in the Stalinist era in their youth, there was a significant generational difference in their outlook. They had few memories of capitalist Poland; it had been a Communist state since they grew up, and they considered socialism a constant factor. As a result, they were more relaxed in their attitudes to ideology. But they were much more demanding with regard to achievements in work performance. They were over-achievers themselves, and they regarded over-achievement as the norm. Their experience in Silesia coloured their outlook:

> They are Communists of a new vintage, less concerned with a distant vision of proletarian paradise than with everyday practical issues. Products of an industrial society, they understand its functioning well; of proletarian background, they are genuinely concerned about bettering the workers' lot. Their exposure to Western influences – not only French and Belgian, but also German (which remains strong in Silesia) – has impressed upon them that the path to improved living standards is improved economic performance.[10]

But the very exposure to foreign influences and lack of exposure to practices in Warsaw proved to be one of the main problems of Gierek's government. Having alienated the old party élite through his appointments, he then proved unable to gain the consensus of the majority of his compatriots to improve their efficiency. Poland, even within its new, more Western borders, has remained an agricultural country. Such a country does not convert easily to an industrial ethos. The population is strongly anti-Communist, though it has periods of honeymoon with new leaders when they provide more goods, but such honeymoons do not last long. Patriotism has been the guiding light of the nation for more than two centuries; and Gierek had no fund of national sympathy to build upon, as had been the case with Gomulka. Moreover, having heard of the Silesian miracle, the population expected to have the same kind of miracle performed throughout the country.

Gierek's biggest problem, however, may have been his

personality. He appeared completely bereft of charismatic qualities. Although a hero to the Silesian miners, he was boring and dreary to the rest of the nation. A bad speaker, his long appearances on television, during which he exhorted the people to be more productive, only exasperated the population. Since half of the Polish population was aged less than twenty-five years, a boring, middle-aged speaker was unlikely to make much progress. As the economic difficulties mounted and the boredom continued, the people began to blame his managerial style. To remedy this, Gierek began to broaden his base of support by drawing some intellectuals into the goverment and administrative posts; he also made efforts to conciliate the Church. But these measures were half-hearted and misunderstood.

Some of Gierek's difficulties were unavoidable and could not have been foreseen. He drew up a plan of rapid industrial expansion with the help of foreign loans; the oil crises of the 1970s frustrated these efforts. Cheap credits were revoked and the country was burdened with a large foreign debt and fewer consumer goods than had been the case under Gomulka. Some analysts accused him of timidity in introducing political and economic reforms similar to those which Kadar introduced in Hungary: 'On the contrary, his largely technocratic approach was posited on the premise of tight central control over essentials.'[11] But this reproach, though partly correct, neglects to take into account the fact that the Polish economy is different from the Hungarian economy, and that the Poles do not act in the same way as the Hungarians do. To have introduced wide-ranging political reforms at this stage (even if Moscow had given the go-ahead) might well have proved explosive. Even without the reforms, the situation was dangerous.

In 1976, the workers began to riot in various parts of the country. Gierek conceded their demands quickly, but the dilemma remained unsolved. It is well known that what had been castigated as Gierek's 'inertia' stemmed from the fact that there was little he could do. The mounting economic problems of the 1970s made the growth of the opposition, both proletarian and intellectual, an almost inevitable certainty. The task was beyond the ageing Gierek, and he knew it. The outcome was almost ritual. Gierek is said to have suffered a heart attack, and the Politburo took advantage of this. It met in an extraordinary session on the night of 5–6 September 1980, and replaced Gierek with Stanislaw Kania, who had apparently been sponsored by Moscow. Gierek left government, unloved and unlamented by party and country. But objective commentators gave him some credit:

> In Communist terms, Gierek was a decent moderately intelligent and realistic liberal-conservative . . . whose compromises satisfied neither the ultras nor the reformers . . . he knew the limits to reform set by the PZPR *apparat* and Soviet power. He was also painfully aware of the combustible nature of Polish society and of the great constraints circumscribing the PZPR's leading role in Poland.[12]

Despite the growing crisis, the party was so unprepared for the event of Gierek's deposition that no likely successor awaited in the wings. Kania was appointed as a stopgap measure, while steps were being taken to contain the growing Solidarity crisis. Yet it took more than a year and a near-revolution for a real successor to emerge. He proved to be astonishingly different and altogether surprising.

A military dictator

Several years after his accession to power, the man who used to be called 'General Zomoza' no longer wore a military uniform, though the dark spectacles were still in evidence.[13] His appearance at a briefing in East Berlin when Mikhail Gorbachev was returning from the Washington summit meeting in December 1987 was almost benign. Yet only a few years earlier, General Jaruzelski had been put in power with only one objective: that of subduing the Solidarity movement and of returning Poland to some form of normality.

The general had had ample practice of subduing opponents of the government in the past, but before his dramatic announcement on the night of 13 December 1981, few people expected that a Communist country would decide to impose a military dictatorship in such an overt manner. That this was done was the index of the panic produced by the Solidarity movement, both in the Polish Politburo and in Moscow. Lessons from the past precluded an invasion; instead, the idea of a military dictatorship arose, possibly invoked by vague memories of Marshal Pilsudski's coup in pre-war Poland.

It was decided that the Poles had to be subdued, but by their own leaders, rather than from the outside.

Initially Jaruzelski's main driving force was seen as his patriotism and several reassuring predictions were drawn up on this basis. Jaruzelski is a Polish aristocrat, one of the few remaining in today's rather proletarian society. But he also boasts impeccable Warsaw Pact credentials. He has been visiting, studying and regularly working in and with the Soviet Union since the age of 12, and his Russian is as fluent as is his Polish.[14]

The military dictatorship was surprising, the background of the dictator was even more so. Jaruzelski's first visit to the Soviet Union was not exactly of a voluntary nature. He is not an aristocrat, but the son of landed gentry, with estates in the Lublin region in central Poland. Born in 1923, he was educated at a Jesuit boarding school, which catered for the sons of landed gentry. Like many middle-class families, the Jaruzelskis were deported to the Soviet Union after the annexation of the eastern part of Poland in September 1939. In 1943, Jaruzelski joined the Polish army under Soviet command and took part in the advance to Poland. After the war he took part in operations against the underground forces opposed to the new regime; these may have been Ukrainian nationalists or the Polish Home Army, though some were genuine bandits. In 1947 he turned to teaching and administration; he became a lecturer in the Higher School of Infantry in Warsaw, and was made the administrative head of military academies. In 1957 he returned to military work and was appointed the commander of an armoured division. In 1965 he went back to administration and became the Chief of General Staff. He had been a deputy minister of defence since 1962, and in 1965 he was promoted to the Ministry of Defence. This military and administrative career finally ended when he was elected First Secretary of the party and appointed prime minister in 1981.

Jaruzelski's party career runs parallel to his military one. He joined the party in 1948, became a member of the Central Committee in 1964, and a member of the Politburo in 1971. He was also deputy chairman of ZBOWID (the veterans' association) from 1972. His administrative and party careers, while revealing much, do not disclose one important fact: that Jaruzelski is considered an expert on guerrilla warfare and crowd control, having taken part in both from a relatively young age. He had fought dissident bands in the early period of the existence of People's Poland; later, in 1970, he was in command of suppressing the Gdansk riots.[15]

His spectacular army and party career notwithstanding, the general seems to be a very ordinary man, though he is no doubt a good administrator. He is married to a university professor, has simple tastes and poor eyesight – hence the dark spectacles. But underneath this simplicity, there is another species of survivor, though of a different kind than Honecker. His exile to the Soviet Union at an early age was a traumatic event, and the conditions were usually appalling. Jaruzelski survived them and, what is more, surmounted them, by joining the Soviet forces rather than opposing them, as might have been expected of a man of his class. He survived the Polish campaign and the skirmishes with dissident bands. He climbed in the ranks of the People's Army at a time when his background should have served to disqualify him. Finally, he survived the disapproval of his countrymen in 1981 and, mainly because of their stubbornness in maintaining the revolt, he became the First Secretary, prime minister and head of government, as well as a military dictator.

Jaruzelski will soon complete ten years of governing the country. In Poland, this has always produced a change of leadership. Since he is reaching the age of retirement, and since there is a trend for younger men to take over, he may well decide to retire soon. However, two factors may keep him in office for a little while longer: in the first place, no one of his stature has yet emerged; and, second, he gets on very well with Mikhail Gorbachev.

Another reason may be that he has begun to display some interest in democratising Poland and in insisting that Polish–Soviet relations be improved. This can only be done by exploring Soviet actions in the Soviet part of the country. Jaruzelski had already condemned the Soviet repression and deportation of Polish civilians after September 1939, as well as the purge of the Polish Communist Party by Stalin in the 1930s. The 'blank spots' needed to be filled in, the two leaders agreed, and a joint Polish–Soviet historical commission was set up to consider the events of the past. This is said to be part of Gorbachev's policy of *glasnost*; but it was also part of Jaruzelski's aim of legitimising his rule. He may yet be seen as the only genuinely patriotic and successful Polish leader of the socialist era.[16]

Notes

1. M.K. Dziewanowski, *Communist Party of Poland*, note 13, p. 340 and p. 169.
2. A. Polonsky and B. Drukier, eds, *The Beginnings of Communist Rule in Poland*, p. 49 and p. 126.
3. Dziewanowski, *Communist Party*, pp. 208–10 and note 5, p. 350.
4. *Ibid.*, pp. 213–14.
5. *Ibid.*, pp. 266–80.
6. A. Ross Johnson, 'Poland: end of an era?', *Problems of Communism*, January–February 1970.
7. George Sanford, *Polish Communism in Crisis*, p. 25.
8. Adam Bromke, 'Poland under Gierek: a new political style', *Problems of Communism*, September–October 1972.
9. Biographical details compiled from the following: Lewytzkyj and Stroynowski, *Kto Jest Kim w Polsce, 1984*, and Bromke, 'Poland under Gierek'.
10. Bromke, 'Poland under Gierek'.
11. Sanford, *Polish Communism*, p. 30.
12. *Ibid.*, p. 41.
13. The name was a compound of the name of Nicaragua's ex-dictator, General Somoza, and the initials of the Polish riot police, ZOMO.
14. 'The secret countdown', *The Sunday Times*, 20 December 1981.
15. *Kto Jest Kim w Polsce, 1984*.
16. 'Jaruzelski criticizes Soviet repression of Polish in 1939', *International Herald Tribune*, 2 September 1987.

7

A monopoly of power

The background to 'dynastic socialism'

In 1976 and early 1977 Romania was preparing to celebrate the centenary of its independence. The culmination of the celebrations took place on 9 May 1977. On that day Nicolae Ceausescu made a speech about the importance and significance of Romania's independence. It must be borne in mind that the event which was being commemorated was the declaration of independence from the Ottoman Empire made by the Romanian principalities – an event which occurred during the Russo-Turkish War of 1877–8. The declaration of independence was formally recognised by the great powers in the Treaty of Berlin in 1878. During the war, some 50,000 Romanian soldiers participated in the Balkan campaign on the side of the Russians, fighting against the Turks. About 10,000 Romanian soldiers died in battle. Since 1945, two other events have been linked with the celebration of Romanian independence from Turkey. The first of these was the anniversary of the founding of the Romanian Communist Party (RCP) on 8 May 1921; and the second was the end of the Second World War on 9 May 1945.[1]

The centenary speech given by the president and party leader was specifically oriented towards the question of nationality. A large segment outlined the history of the Romanians from the time of the Dacians, some two thousand years ago, until the current period. Ceausescu had treated Romanian history in this manner before. At the Congress of Culture in 1976 he had portrayed the party as the culmination of a lengthy process of historical development. He also reiterated that the Romanians were descended from the Dacians, and that they had inherited their determination to maintain their independence and territorial integrity from those highly civilised ancestors. He then stated that the anniversary of the foundation of the first independent centralised Dacian state under Burebista, over two thousand years earlier, on the territory of present-day Romania, would be suitably commemorated. These allusions to ancient history were intended to prove the continuity of the Romanian people's presence in the region, in contrast to the 'migratory waves' of Hungarians, Germans, Slavs, Tartars and others. Ceausescu maintained that the Romanians had never lost their desire to maintain their autonomy. 'Unlike the other peoples of the Danube Basin who were integrated into the Ottoman or the Hapsburg Empire, the Romanian people never entirely lost their independence, and they succeeded in maintaining true state autonomy.' A postscript to the story of maintaining independence was the comment that, in return for financial dues, the Turks agreed not to interfere in Romania's internal affairs and to protect the country against external attacks.[2]

On the international scene, said the president in his speech, the war of independence had strengthened Romania's relations with Russia, creating 'solidarity and military brotherhood between Romanian and Russian soldiers'. And because of help given by the Bulgarians, the Romanians had also developed bonds with the Bulgarian people. All the Balkan peoples, the Greeks, the Serbs and the Albanians, have also allied with Romania which, in its turn, supported their struggle for national liberation. After the democratisation of Turkey under Kemal Attaturk, the Romanians also developed friendly ties with the Turkish Republic. Romania's experience, said Ceausescu, was that, when a people decide to defend their territory and their freedom, they cannot be defeated or subjugated by anyone at any time. Hence, 'a state that follows a policy of domination and oppression and disregards or violates the elementary rights of other peoples, no matter how strong its military forces may be, is eventually doomed to defeat'.[3]

Though the gist of the speech was that true independence in Romania had begun only after political power had been seized by the working classes, it gave away, perhaps subconsciously, the core of the argument: that is, the uniqueness of the Romanian experience. This is well substantiated. While the Romanians are a Balkan nation, they do not belong to any of the major clans (Dacians apart, which, even if true, belongs to distant history); as a result they suffer from a lack of national identity and try to identify with an ancient tribe in order to maintain their national pride. National identity is even more difficult to maintain in Romania in view of its social cleavages. While in modern times the ruling élite, with Ceausescu and his family at the head, is divided from the other classes, in the past, in pre-socialist Romania, the split was even deeper. Before the advent of the Communists, the divisions were related to wealth, social standing, education, traditions and even language. In the socialist state, the division is maintained between the privileged élite party members and the not-so-privileged person in the street.

Forced to live in a kind of limbo among the Balkan clans which are relatively cohesive, the Romanians have always tried to compensate for it in other ways. The alliance with Nazi Germany and the invasion of the USSR was an attempt to gain importance and influence. When this attempt failed, Romania tried to fight Germany on the side of the Soviet Union. With the war finally over, and the monarchy re-etablished, the Communists had to work hard to unseat the king. They managed it finally, despite Stalin's opposition, and a Communist regime was established. Having arrived at this high point, the Romanian party then began to indulge in internecine warfare and a series of purges more ferocious than in any other socialist state. Eventually, when the ascendant group, led by Gheorgiu Dej, gained power, it refused to allow anyone else a share in the power.

These developments affected Romania's political course after the death of Stalin. Dej had not been a convinced Stalinist right from the start. Indeed, he had initially supported Tito in his efforts to create a Balkan federation, and only condemned those plans when Stalin began to distrust them. But Stalinism began to suit him, particularly after Stalin's death. In 1957 Dej purged Miron Constantinescu, on the grounds that he may have been designated by Khrushchev to be his successor. Ceausescu continued his predecessor's policies, and purged anyone who disagreed with him. The one constant aim of Romanian leaders seems to have been the removal of hypothetical opponents; the building of Communism comes second. It has been suggested that the 'nationalist' line lies at the bottom of the continuing power struggle:

> This brings us to the problem of pinpointing the origins of the Romanian national deviation. . . . Both the date of origin and the causes of the deviation have been a matter of some controversy. There are those who trace it as far back as 1955, the year when the Romanian Workers' (Communist) Party first began to claim exclusive credit for Romania's wartime switch to the side of the Allies, implying their early independence from the Soviet Union.[4]

The refusal of the Romanian leadership to follow Khrushchev's directives could have had dire consequences. The implications of the purge of Constantinescu and Chisinevsky in 1957 were sufficiently grave in themselves, but there were also 'reports – albeit unsubstantiated – of a Soviet-inspired conspiracy against Dej in the fall of 1962, involving the party leader, Emil Bodnaras. However tenuous the evidence, all the factors point to the likelihood of tension, rather than co-operation, in the Khrushchev–Dej relationship,' commented one author.[5] However, even if these reports were true, it must have been decided in the Kremlin that the Romanian party's position was so marginal in the Bloc that the Russians could afford to leave it alone. And possibly because of this, as well as the fact that Khrushchev was deposed soon afterwards, Gheorgiu Dej survived Soviet disapproval and in due course transferred the leadership to Nicolae Ceausescu.

It was Ceausescu who, armed with Communist and nationalist principles, began to run an independent foreign policy. This was facilitated by Dej's policies before he left power. At the time of his death in March 1965, Dej combined the roles of First Secretary of the party and of president. He had fought Khruschev with success on the issues of economic integration of the Comecon and had started a policy of improving relations with the West. He had also begun to establish closer ties with China, Albania and Yugoslavia, all of whom had some areas of disagreement with the Soviet Union. 'Internally, Dej initiated a process of cultural de-Russification and Romanianization which mobilized the masses behind the regime and its new foreign policy.' Ceausescu followed the broad outlines of Dej's policy, limiting the degree of participation in the Warsaw Pact and the Comecon, while expanding his relations with the West. As one commentator noted:

Ceausescu's most notable contribution has been in the realm of personal diplomacy. Beginning in 1969, he initiated a series of personal visits to heads of state in both the Communist and non-Communist worlds, and the number of world leaders visiting Bucharest also increased.[6]

This policy of independence of the Soviet policy was a personal creation of Dej, and was followed and expanded by Ceausescu. Nowhere else in Eastern Europe have Communist leaders played such a decisive role in shaping an independent policy, and nowhere have they succeeded in staying in power, should they attempt it. How and why this happened in Romania is still not clearly understood, but it may have been related to the Romanian feelings of exclusivity, as well as to a sense of grievance arising out of Soviet exploitation of Romania, and of the annexation of its rich provinces at the end of the Second World War. However, other Bloc countries were also exploited and had territory annexed, yet none made such a strong stand against the Russians. This unusual situation may have arisen out of the Romanian feelings of separateness, as well as out of the character of their leaders.

The leader and the family

Nicolae Ceausescu was born in January 1918, the son of a peasant family in a Romanian province. He moved to Bucharest in 1931 in order to learn a trade, and joined the then illegal Union of Communist Youth (UCY) in 1933. He joined the Communist Party in 1936. In the same year he was sentenced to two and a half years in prison, and spent the period in the Brasov and Doftana prisons. After release, he obtained a degree from the Academy of Economic studies in Bucharest. He was again sentenced to three years in prison in 1939; this time *in absentia*, but he was arrested in 1940, and sent to two other prisons, and finally, to the notorious Tirgu Jiu internment camp.

He was appointed secretary of the UCY after the liberation of Romania in August 1944, and from then on continued his steady climb in the party hierarchy, until he became the party leader, head of state and chairman of the Defence Council in 1965, 1967 and 1969 respectively.[7] This apparently effortless ascent was a much more complicated exercise than would appear from the brief biography outlined above. While in the process of the climb Ceausescu became a symbolic, almost charismatic figure in the country; but to begin with, he was virtually insignificant. 'An unprepossessing and almost unknown figure during the rule of his predecessor, Ceausescu assumed office as head of the Party in 1965. . . . At the time, he was the youngest Party leader in East Europe.' When he succeeded to office, Ceausescu was forty-seven years old, and was forced to share power with a number of Gheorgiu Dej's associates for two years. By December 1967, however, he was elected chairman of the Council of State (titular head of state), and in 1974 the office of 'President of the Republic' was created especially for him.[8]

Though Ceausescu enjoyed a period of popularity, particularly in the West, because of his independent stand, his image was not generally favourable. One analyst noted that he had acquired supreme power, and liked to show it. He was even presented with a sceptre, a symbol of power in Imperial Rome. However, though he liked to appear as an independent Communist leader in the West, it did not compensate for the fact that

> he leans on and serves the long-term objectives in Moscow. Moscow will tolerate his 'independence' but he is at the mercy of the men in the Kremlin, who are moved by Communism, while at the same time at the mercy of the support he can get from the people in his own party, who are moved by nationalism.

Further complaints were made that Ceausescu had a mediocre intellect and little ability to communicate; even his best friends joked about his poor delivery and his bad pronunciation. But these faults seem to have had little negative influence on the building up of his own personality cult: 'He is already referred to in the controlled Communist press as the greatest Romanian in all history, going back to our ancestors, the Dacians.'[9]

It is often said that behind every successful man there is a talented woman. If Ceausescu is not particularly good-looking or charismatic, his wife, Elena, makes up for it. A handsome, well-dressed and ambitious woman, she has climbed through the ranks, like her husband, and has made a niche for herself in the country's cultural and political institutions. She is said to dress in Paris, and to require the most luxurious articles. While her husband is modest in his personal demands, Elena Ceausescu is his exact opposite. Elena Ceausescu's influence cannot be discounted, because in this – the most Balkan of all Balkan countries – it appears that it is the women who make most policies, albeit behind closed doors.

A Romanian exile, who used to be a high party official, tells the story of events during the immediate post-war years, when most of the Communist leaders had little or no formal education, and there were many ministerial posts to fill.

> Their solution was ingenious, though a comical one. Many of them left their wives, who in any case were getting on in years, and married young intellectuals, usually their secretaries, with a sound education and knowledge of foreign langauges. As it happened, a lot of them were Jewish. This is in the 1946–47 period. . . . Twelve years later, after the famous plenary session of the Central Committee in 1958, these oligarchs left their wives *en masse* because the policy at that time was decidedly anti-semitic. Again they married their young secretaries.

An unofficial estimate at that time was that the average age of the senior officials was fifty-four, while that of their wives was twenty-five.[10]

Though an educated and young wife may be the main prop of Romanian leaders, the tradition of nepotism dies hard in a Balkan country. The families of the leaders expect and get handsome dividends from their senior relatives. Many members of Ceausescu's family are in high government and party positions; it was noted that 'All of Ceausescu's six brothers are in positions of power.'[11] Nepotism apart, the élites stay united out of necessity; to remove one member would mean the removal of all his dependants, and, whatever the drawbacks of this system, a cohesiveness has been established which, while precluding the entry of strangers into the hierarchy, also bolsters stability. To an outsider, the system may appear corrupt; but there is no guarantee that in Romania any other system would have been less corrupt.

Since the Romanian leadership successfully established the rule of one family, it remains to enquire whether this has made its position so strong that it could persist in its 'independence' of the Soviet Union, and be indifferent to the views of the CPSU. Some analysts, particularly those with close Romanian connections, provide an explanation, if only a partial one, of the Romanian party's stance, particularly with regard to its special brand of nationalism.

The roots of Ceausescu's nationalism

According to this school of thought, Ceausescu's philosophy is due to the unusual circumstances in which the party was created and to the way in which it had influenced his life. It was noted that 'The political order prevailing in Romania today, which can be labelled incipient "dynastic socialism", cannot be explained without taking into account the personality of Nicolae Ceausescu, who dominates the country's public life.' He installed numerous members of his family in key posts of the party and state apparatuses and under-mined the institutional role of the party. He also increasingly inter-preted both the history of the Romanian Communist movement and the role of socialism in Romania in his own manner. His interpretation seems to have been to impose neo-Stalinism at home, and neo-Titoism abroad. If one amplifies this point, it could be said that Romania's politics have been of a highly personalised nature, the personality of Ceausescu being all-pervasive.[12]

If Ceausescu has identified the history of the party with his own personality, the reason may lie in the fact that the party was very small when he joined it, and that he was very young when he became a member. These two phenomena may have become inter-mingled in his mind. Paradoxically, in view of the party's national-ism, the Romanian Communist Party was not an indigenous one, but was almost entirely the creation of the Comintern, which im-posed its policies and personnel on it. Ceausescu joined the youth section of the party in 1933, at the age of fifteen, when it was an illegal organisation. In the same year the party gained some pres-tige, when Gheorgiu Dej organised a strike in a railroad workshop. On 1 May 1939, the party organised a demonstration against the Fascist Iron Guard organisation. As a result, many activists were arrested and jailed. Ceausescu himself was not apprehended till 1940, but when arrested, he remained in prison until the liberation of the country by Soviet troops in 1944.

Though the RCP was small and illegal in the 1930s, it began to attract many intellectuals who had become alarmed by the growing strength of the Iron Guard, and who were dissatisfied with the policies of King Carol II. Possibly because of the support of the intellectuals, Gheorgiu Dej became the focus of opposition to the government's policy, and his popularity rivalled that of the elected general secretary, who was the Comintern's choice. It may have been his popularity which was responsible for the fact that while many Communists who had been arrested with Dej were released, or had had escapes from prison arranged for them, he remained jailed till 1944. It is said that 'some . . . ascribe Dej's intense dislike for the Comintern and some of the RCP leaders to the fact that Dej was among the few prominent activists whose rescue from jail was never arranged'.[13]

Dej's dislike of the Russians and the Comintern may also be ascribed to the way in which foreign leaders, first Polish, then Hungarian, were imposed on the Romanian party by the Comintern. And it can also be due to the Stalinist purges of the Romanian Communists in the 1930s, when many Romanians were either imprisoned or executed. If an additional reason were needed, one can add the annexation of Bessarabia and Northern Bukovina by the Soviet Union. Wartime relations with the CPSU were not on a good footing either. Instead of direct communications, the Romanian party received its directives through the consulate in Varna; this slight did not improve relations.

During the period of Dej's imprisonment, the Hungarian leader of the Romanian party, Stefan Foris, found the 'centre of prisons' led by Dej and Ceausescu, a serious problem. It is believed that at this time, the party suffered from dual leadership. Eventually, in early 1944, when victory was in sight, two of Stalin's trusted agents, Emil Bodnaras and Constantin Pirvulescu, were sent to Romania to report on the situation. They recommended that Foris be removed, and Dej installed as general secretary. 'Dej, an ethnic Romanian, benefited from Moscow's decision to build up the national base of the RCP so as to counteract the negative impression created by the dominance of foreigners in the party leadership.' With an impending victory and the Romanian oil reserves in mind, the party suddenly became more important to Moscow, and its future was being reconsidered. But it was a very chequered party. Bodnaras himself was an interesting example of the mixture of various elements in the party. While he was an officer in the Royal Romanian Army, he was exposed as a Soviet agent, and had to defect to the Soviet Union. During the war, he returned to the country in order to organise anti-Nazi commando units. He later became one of the chief architects of Dej's autonomous policy, and was, subsequently, one of Ceausescu's closest advisers.[14]

The diversified nature of the party was further enhanced when Romania switched her alliances in August 1944. Dej's domestic party was merged with the Communists returning from Moscow. Ana Pauker and Vasile Luca, together with Dej and Georgescu, became the RCP's four ruling leaders. Foris was disposed of very quickly. He was removed from leadership, accused of treason to the revolutionary movement, and executed without a trial in 1946. The vengeance of the new leadership did not stop there. Foris's mother was assassinated, while his wife was arrested and convicted as her husband's accomplice. She survived her prison sentence and was invited to speak at a meeting of the Bucharest party cadres in April 1968, when Foris was rehabilitated. It can be seen that, apart from its enmity towards the CPSU, the Romanian leadership exhibited unusual ferocity towards anyone who threatened its power. Internecine struggle continued for a long time and went on even after Dej died. This demonstrated that the struggle was institutional, not personal, though it did rely on the ruthless characters of the leaders, who were prepared to do almost anything to remain in power.

Despite Soviet disapproval, Dej continued to purge his hypothetical opponents until the mid-1950s. His last rival, Patrascanu, was not executed until 1954, a year after Stalin's death. 'Dej and his adherents feared Patrascanu as a potential catalyst for an anti-Stalinist reaction in the party that could challenge their position. Moreover, they feared that he could be used as a political card by the Soviets in their search for an alternative solution in Eastern Europe.' Since Ceausescu was not a member of the Politburo when Patrascanu's execution was endorsed, he later capitalised on his presumed innocence in order to discredit Dej's policies. Nevertheless, Ceausescu clearly benefited by the purges carried out by Dej, particularly after Ana Parker and Luca were removed from the leadership in 1952, and he rose in the hierarchy. In 1955 Ceausescu made his first major political speech, giving a report on the modification of party rules at the Second Congress of the RWP(RCP).[15]

From that year on, Ceausescu was the obvious heir apparent. He supported Dej in every respect: in his opposition to de-Stalinisation, in his renewed purges of the party in 1956 and later, in his condemnation of those purged as right-wing deviationists. The speech against Ana Pauker and other former leaders, which Ceausescu made in December 1961, helped to further his career even more. He was appointed the chief of the Organisational Directorate, which included the supervision of 'special organs', that is, the security police, the military and the judiciary. When Dej decided to negotiate a truce in the Sino–Soviet dispute in the 1960s, Ceausescu was sent, in 1964, to China, North Korea and the Soviet Union in order to pursue the negotiations.

Dej had been ill for some time before his death in March 1965, and Ceausescu ran the secretariat during this period. He was elected general secretary in March of that year when he began to demonstrate liberal and anti-Stalinist views. He suggested changing the name of the party back to that of the Romanian Communist Party (a symbolic gesture), and at a Central Committee plenum in May 1965, rehabilitated several party members whom Dej had purged. Perhaps even more significantly, he supported the 'outspoken criticism of the Russification of Romanian culture'. It has been pointed out that Ceausescu followed the Khrushchevian tradition of blaming individuals for transgressions of 'socialist legality', and exonerated himself as someone who had had no part in those transgressions.

The apex of Ceausescu's liberal phase came in 1968. He removed Alexandru Draghici from the party and state apparatus, blaming him for personal responsibility in Patrascanu's execution in 1954, and made a strong stand against the Warsaw Pact's intervention in Czechoslovakia. 'Ceausescu's reaction was public and vehement: a rally was held in the Palace Square in Bucharest, and the Romanian leader described the invasion as "a great mistake and a grave danger to peace . . . a shameful moment in the history of the revolutionary movement".'[16] He also stated unequivocally that the Romanian people would not allow anybody to violate the territory of their country. He was supported in these sentiments by the whole nation, to whom the idea of yet another Soviet occupation was abhorrent. There were some rumours of an imminent Soviet invasion of Romania, but they do not appear to have had any substance. However, if the Russians did contemplate an invasion, (partly because of Romania's stand on the Czech invasion, and partly for logistic reasons), it could be that Ceausescu's strong stand deterred such a move, because it could easily have ended in bloodshed. It was commented:

> Romanian resistance could hardly have been effective for long against combined action by members of the Warsaw Pact, but military occupation would have demanded a great many troops. Whatever the truth about Soviet intentions, the Romanian population perceived danger, and Ceausescu received the credit for averting invasion.[17]

However, there were deeper reasons for Ceausescu's stand than simple opposition to Soviet interference. If the Russians had invaded Romania, he would certainly have been deposed, just as Dubcek was deposed. Therefore he had nothing to lose by showing opposition. By the same token, his show of independence increased his popularity in the country much more than any economic or diplomatic successes. If Ceausescu's behaviour was based on these premises, then he proved to be a very good tactician. The dangers and benefits of such tactics would have had to be carefully evaluated; and the danger of defeat could not be discounted. At this point, in 1968, Ceausescu won, and gained admiration among the population. But it was the last instance of growing popularity. From that time on, matters began to deteriorate.

How to become an idol

Ceausescu's problems began with his handling of the Romanian economy. Although this question will not be examined here, comment is made on his personal mistakes in relation to the economic situation in Romania. At the Tenth Party Congress in 1969, Ceausescu announced new economic goals, which he knew would cause discontent in the country. Some writers ascribe the building of the cult of personality to this factor. Because the economic goals were impossible to attain, and because the leader had no gift of communicating with the masses, a cult of personality had to be constructed to make the people obey orders. 'When Ceausescu faces a large crowd, he becomes awkward and retreats into formality, reading speeches in a monotone . . with the stress all too often falling on the wrong word. . . . Ceausescu could not lead the masses, and so had to fool them,' commented one analyst. This comment explains part of the difficulty, but by no means all of it.[18]

The most serious challenge encountered by Ceausescu came from the Romanian intelligentsia. Significant change could not be effected without the intellectuals; but the intellectuals found their leader dull and unconvincing and refused to co-operate. After a visit to China in 1971, Ceausescu became convinced that a mini-cultural revolution would cure the liberal tendencies of the intellectuals. By November 1971, he had begun to attack liberalism within the party, and managed to maintain a policy of cultural freeze thereafter. Simultaneously, he eradicated much of Soviet influence from Romanian life – not so much because of his evident dislike of the Russians, but because he wanted to be able to carry out his plans without Soviet interference. He was assisted in this by the fact that the Russians, aware that Romania was completely locked inside the Socialist Bloc, were fairly passive. The Soviet response was also muted, because it was believed that the Romanian army would not fight against the Soviet army, and because there was little concern for the oppressed Romanian population. Besides, the Romanians were a useful channel of communication with the West, and Romania was the only country in the Bloc to maintain diplomatic relations with Israel. This suited the Soviet policy of retaining a channel of communications, however indirect, with a state which was officially condemned.

A Romanian defector who had been deputy chief of the intelligence service and a personal adviser to Ceausescu has questioned whether the leader had any pro-Israeli feelings. He came to the conclusion that the relations depended on hard cash. According to his testimony, millions of dollars were paid to Ceausescu in return for permits for emigration for Romanian Jews. If this information is correct, then it involved a change of policy, because when Ceausescu came to power in 1965, he ended the practice of charging fees for Jewish emigration. However, two years later, when the government was short of cash, the payments had to be resumed again. The defector claimed that the government used a sliding scale, charging higher prices if the prospective emigrant had special skills or secret information. The intelligence services were 'laundering the money. Every single dollar was exchanged in Zurich.' After 1972, a similar operation was worked out for ethnic Germans, and by 1978 the two combined had brought in more than 400 million US dollars. The defector also maintained that there was no close relationship between Romania and Israel; on the contrary, 'Mr Ceausescu had a warm personal regard for Mr Arafat. . . . The Romanians gave the group blank passports and intelligence support.' Ceausescu's closest friends were said to be Yasser Arafat and the Libyan leader, Colonel Gaddafi. Even a joint Romanian–Libyan tank, financed by Libyan money, was planned.[19]

Aided by Soviet indifference or tacit approval, Ceausescu was able to build up an empire for himself and his family. 'Ceausescu has the most personalized style of rule among East European leaders. Indeed, according to Trond Gilberg, the "most important decisions in Romania today are being made in response to Ceausescu's personal initiative. . . . The apparatchiks either wait for an initiative from the general secretary or attempt to anticipate his wishes." '[20] Opposition is paralysed by the active and numerous political police and the present élite shows few signs of wishing to dissent.

Ceausescu and his family are in total charge of all aspects of Romanian policy. As of last count, some fifty members of his family were in senior positions in the party and the government, including his wife, son and brothers.[21] His main partner in power is his wife, Elena Petrescu, whom he married in 1939 while they were both activists in the Union of Communist Youth. As noted earlier, Mrs Ceausescu is a striking and intelligent woman who accompanies her husband on many of his official engagements. She is also a highly qualified chemical engineer, and holds several important party and scientific posts. She has, in the last few years, been accorded the same amount of adulation as her husband. The couple have three children: Nicu, Valentin and Zoia, but only Nicu has political ambitions; the other two are scientists. Nicu, born in 1951, has made steady progress in the party and his wife is the head of the Young Pioneer organisation.

Until the arrival of Mikhail Gorbachev on the Soviet scene, it appeared that the 'dynasty' would survive Ceausescu's death, with power probably being shared by Elena and Nicu. But Gorbachev's attempts to modernise the Bloc and bring its economy back into equilibrium may have ruined their chances. Ceausescu plunged Romania into complete chaos and disruption with his economic and social policies, and his nepotistic style of government does not suit the image of modernism which Gorbachev wants to impose on the Bloc. Romania's feud with the neighbouring Hungary has also embarrassed the Soviet Union. Ceausescu, aged and ill, refuses to consider any changes.

> The 70-year-old Rumanian Communist Party leader, who has ruled unchallenged for 23 years, was described . . . as totally convinced of the correctness and ideological purity of his policies. They said only his wife, Elena, appeared to have any influence over him, and her views coincided with her husband's.[22]

Owing to Ceausescu's age and state of health, and the structural changes in the Bloc, the situation is bound to be resolved in the near future. Its outcome will be considered later on in this work.

Notes

1. RFE Research, *Romania/16*, Situation Report, 12 May 1977.
2. *Ibid.*
3. *Ibid.*
4. R.V. Burks, 'Romania and a theory of progress', *Problems of Communism*, May–June 1972.
5. Burks, 'Romania'.
6. Robert L. Farlow, 'Romanian foreign policy: a case of partial alignment', *Problems of Communism*, November–December 1971.
7. *Who's Who in Socialist Countries.*
8. Mary Ellen Fischer, 'Idol or leader? The origins and the future of the Ceausescu cult', in D.N. Nelson, *Romania in the 1980s.*
9. Ion Ratiu, *Contemporary Romania*, pp. 106–7.
10. *Ibid.*, p. 109.
11. *Ibid.*, p. 111. A slightly different count is given in Narkiewicz, *Eastern Europe*, p. 265.
12. Vladimir Tismaneanu, 'Ceausescu's socialism', *Problems of Communism*, January–February 1985.
13. *Ibid.*
14. *Ibid.* A brief, 'unofficial' history of the RCP can also be found in this work.
15. Tismaneanu, 'Ceausescu's socialism'.
16. Fischer, *Idol or Leader?*, pp. 123–5.
17. *Ibid.*, p. 125.
18. *Ibid.*, p. 127. A brief account of Romania's economic difficulties will be found in Narkiewicz, *Eastern Europe*, particularly Chapter 2.
19. 'Rumanian recalls deal for emigrés', *New York Times*, 14 October 1987.
20. Tismaneanu, 'Ceausescu's socialism'. On various aspects of the cult of personality, see Fischer, *Idol or Leader?*, pp. 127–33.

21. See 'Can Romania's family rule on?', *The Sunday Times*, 26 August 1984, and Narkiewicz, *Eastern Europe*, p. 265.
22. 'For Bucharest, a great leap backward', *New York Times*, 15 February 1988. On the Romanian–Hungarian feud, see 'Ceausescu refuses to yield on reforms', *The Guardian*, 30 August 1988.

8

The leaders and the nations

General effects of the 'leadership' syndrome

So far, this work has conducted a systematic survey of leaders in the six countries of the Socialist Bloc, and has demonstrated striking dissimilarities, both in the style of leadership and in the national reactions to those styles. Since the survey was carried out over a length of time, some four decades, it was expected that there would be several changes of leaders in each country. This was not the case. In several countries the leadership only changed once; in others, owing either to purges or to disorders, the change-over was much more frequent.

It is obvious that where there were frequent changes in the leadership the reason was not difficult to see: matters were not going well. But it is questionable whether in the countries where the leadership maintained its position for a long period, matters were conducted better; or whether their continuation in power depended simply on greater apathy among the people, or on stronger police powers. However, one factor is certain – that is, that the conditions in each of the countries examined, and in the Bloc as a whole, played a large role in the leaders' success or lack of it.

The conditions, as is well known, were conducive neither to good government, nor a well-run economy. The government of the East European countries would have proved difficult for any leadership, whether Communist or not. Towards the end of the century, in the prosperous parts of the world, it is easy to forget how underdeveloped these countries were before the war, and how ruined they had been during the war. Given a team of managerial geniuses and large amounts of capital and manpower, some progress might have been made. None of these were available. Assessing the state of Eastern Europe recently, one writer noted:

> Poland's social fabric had been torn to shreds by five years of German occupation, and a new political system was constructed under the guns of the Red Army. The attempt by Churchill and Roosevelt at Yalta to create a Poland in the image of their own societies was doomed to fail; liberal parliamentary government had no roots here. The same is true of the other East and Central European countries that were occupied by Soviet forces, with the exception of Czechoslovakia. In all the others, various types of totalitarian regimes had been in power in the prewar period. None of them had had much practice with holding free and unfettered elections.[1]

To the social and political difficulites must be added the devastation in housing, transport, agriculture, industry and education, which both the war and the Nazi policies caused. Nor can the fact be overlooked that the Nazis aimed at drastically reducing the educated strata in these countries in order to create a pliable work force. In some cases, as in Poland, the loss was almost irreplaceable.[2] In those circumstances, most politicians might be inclined to despair and give up. It must be to the credit of the new leaderships after 1945 that they persisted, though not, of course, without the persuasion provided by Soviet bayonets. However, persistence is probably the only positive feature of those early leaderships. The rest of their record is so dismal that it makes sad reading, not only because of the harm they caused, but also because of the opportunities they missed. Their successors were often more civilised in their approach to government, but less able to govern, partly because the element of terror had been reduced, and partly because they themselves were, in general, simply mediocre functionaries.

There is reason to believe that the choice of mediocrities was to some extent deliberate. Talented people tend to be innovative, and innovation could spell danger to the system, as well as to the major partner in the Bloc. But the rest of the problem consisted in the fact that there was also a dearth of able people in all the countries concerned, and that those who were still available were either considered politically untrustworthy, or refused to co-operate with the socialist governments. The mediocre personalities had one virtue: they were all loyal Communists who often believed what they preached, and who were obedient to Soviet dictates. Nevertheless, even the ablest leaders could have done little in countries which were ruined by the war, which had a new political system imposed on them from abroad, and in which there was no political opposition, no political freedom, and a total physical dependence on their large neighbour, both in internal and external policies.

To complicate matters further, the leaders had to appear all-powerful within their own countries, while at the same time submitting unconditionally to the Soviet leadership. The situation was such that, on the one hand, the nations had to be led to believe that their leaders acted independently, while on the other hand the CPSU had to be assured of total loyalty to the Soviet cause. There were also problems about relations with non-Communist countries, on which a harmonised policy was not worked out for several years; and later on, as the Bloc began to break down, other problems in relations with socialist countries at odds with the policy of the CPSU. The solution to such problems required a great deal of flexibility, duplicity and diplomacy. Under the circumstances, it is perhaps little wonder that many of the leaders suffered from coronary disease, and that some succumbed to strokes in moments of crisis. There was a definite occupational risk for all the leaders, even after the risk of summary executions had been reduced. The available evidence does not show that the leaders were aware of the risk, but ill-health, or the threat of ill-health, does not seem to have encouraged them to give up power. Even had they been willing to leave their posts, their position was not similar to that of leaders in parliamentary systems; so far as is known, they were unable to leave their posts unless they were deposed. There were many reasons for this: some of them were due to the rigidity of the system, which did not provide for replacements, and some were due to the special privileges which went with the posts, and to the difficult conditions which they would have to face if they resigned. In the final analysis, East European leaderships were trapped in a set of circumstances over which they had little or no control, and which were not of their own making. Similarly, the population of those countries was trapped in a different set of circumstances, imposed from above, and resented by most. Such a situation did not provide good grounds for orderly and reasonable government.

Nevertheless, over the decades, socialist governments did improve, particularly in comparison to the early, Stalinist period. The Stalinist leaders have not been the subject of this work, though they were surveyed very briefly at the outset, because some reference to their personalities had to be taken into account; this was necessary in order to demonstrate the extent of the change in practice once Stalinism had been phased out.

It has been seen that the Stalinist leaders were Communists who had spent long periods of time either in Moscow, or working for the Comintern, often moving from country to country. Many of them had working-class backgrounds; or, if they came from the middle classes, they had abandoned their middle-class life-styles. Most of them had spent some periods of time in various prisons; many had spent long periods in concentration camps. The majority returned to Moscow, where they attended party schools or university courses. These young people witnessed the purges of their senior colleagues in the 1930s, and those who escaped being purged must have felt very fortunate. The war between Germany and the USSR provided a chance for them to prove their loyalty and prepare the ground for a return to their own countries. They now devoted themselves to carrying out propaganda work in the media, and waited until they were summoned to return.

It can be seen that though their experience was varied, and many had travelled widely, their vision was narrow. The extent of their relations with the public at large was limited, and their work was reduced to dealing with internal party problems. Their freedom of action was constrained by Stalin's policies, and they often had serious problems relating to their own countries. This was enhanced by the fact that they had spent long periods of time in exile, and that at a crucial time – during the Second World War – they did not share in their compatriots' hardships and dangers. They thus developed a detached attitude towards their own countries – almost as though their native countries were foreign. In many cases, either because their families were Russian, or because they had become attached to their adoptive country, they appear to have felt more at home in the Soviet Union than in their native land.

This factor played one of the most important roles in attitudes after the war. The second factor was even more crucial. All these leaders who came to power in the Bloc after the war had survived Stalinist purges, and some had suffered during them. While it is doubtful that they were of a sensitive nature before these events (otherwise would they have supported Stalin?), such a long exposure to the horrifying experiences which their colleagues and friends underwent was bound to inure them to all forms of terror. Once they had acquired power, they did not hesitate to behave in the same manner as the Soviet secret police had behaved during the purges. The use of terror, apart from being institutionalised, was also due to the fact that they had few intellectual resources, and could find no better way to govern than through instilling fear. These two main factors, together with other, additional ones, combined to make the Stalinist leaders not only cruel, but crude. At times one is inclined to think, when considering their actions, that their thought patterns had been completely wiped out, like a recording erased from a tape, and that a substitution had been made with a Stalinist-recorded programme.

The next generation of leaders was rather different. Though many of them, men like Honecker, Gomulka and Husak, had spent some time in anti-Communist prisons, they did so as young activists. They also escaped Stalinist persecution because of their junior status, and came to top posts almost by default, because the older generation had been removed. Their accession to power was faciliated by the fact that, between them, Stalin and Hitler had wiped out and eradicated the most able Communist leaders, and, consequently, the road to promotion was wide open for minor personalities. There was also some difference in their educational standards. Though most of them came from working-class backgrounds, leaders like Gomulka, Ceausescu and Zhivkov had acquired some education, often at university level. Another difference was that they had often worked in the underground in their own countries, particularly during the war, and thus had little experience of Moscow – less, certainly, than the previous leaders. Many had escaped exposure to the worst aspects of Stalinism, though they had all worked for Stalinist leaders in their youth and had, perforce, acquired some Stalinist characteristics. Finally, they came to power in slightly more relaxed circumstances, in a period when Soviet power in Eastern Europe was consolidated, and they could afford to be more relaxed themselves as a result.

Perhaps the most important feature of the new leaders' personalities was the fact that they had had fewer problems than the previous ones, and that they had had the opportunity to acquire, together with better education, a taste for different life-styles. While the earlier leaders may have lived in luxury in their guarded fortresses or castles, they were almost barbaric in their attitudes. The new leaders did not always reject luxury, particularly when their wives demanded it, but, by and large, they had a middle-class life-style and middle-class outlook. Often, as in the case of Zhivkov, Honecker and Ceausescu, their wives or children exhibited a strong interest in culture and education. They attended the theatre and the opera, read books and learned foreign languages. Their clothes were well made and their figures were trim. They could easily have passed for senior civil servants in a West European country, and their outlook was not dissimilar to that of an average senior civil servant.

This, in reality, is what they were. With the eradication of bloodbaths and show trials and the establishment of a more stable system of government, they had fewer fears and more confidence in themselves than any previous Communist leaders. They were also more constrained by the new guidelines on 'collective rule', and, although they wielded a lot of power, such power was limited by peer pressure. This change, together with the continuing need to conform with most of the CPSU's policies (though in a less slavish fashion than before), made them conservative and unwilling to take risks. It provided a new pattern of Communist government – one led by men whose functions were obvious, but whose powers were not altogether established.

The influence of national characteristics

The result of these changes implied that the new leaders were, for the most part, sailing in uncharted waters. Just as the leaders of the Hungarian revolt in 1956, and the leaders of the Czechoslovak Reform movement in 1968 did not know the limits of their freedom of action, but found out, in a rough-and-ready fashion, when they overstepped the mark, so the new leaders were uncertain of how far they could go, either with a view to repression or to liberalisation.

Much depended on the contemporaneous Soviet leadership and the trend of the CPSU's policies. In many ways, the leaders must have longed for the predictable period of Stalinism, when it was at least known where to stop, or even whether not to start at all. Even after Stalinism was phased out, the Brezhnev doctrine provided a welcome framework for their actions, particularly after 1968; as the invasion of Czechoslovakia proved to be a firm statement of 'dos' and 'don'ts' in the Socialist Bloc. But from the moment of Brezhnev's last illness until the installation of Mikhail Gorbachev – and even more so thereafter – the rules were uncertain, changeable and possibly even non-existent.

Because of this fluid state, the leaders in power took refuge in 'national interest', or in the concept of 'stability'. Though the former could be interpreted as chauvinism and the latter as *immobilisme*, and though this was often the correct conclusion, the rulers could hardly be blamed for adopting such defensive tactics. In the circumstances, their choice was very limited. As a result of these policies, the Romanians were told to take pride in their Dacian origins; a claim as removed from reality as that of the Albanians being descended from the ancient Illyrians. These claims were supported by statements that the other nations in the region were illegitimate occupants of countries which should rightfully be inhabited by one particular nationality. A particularly revealing letter about Albanian claims to the province of Kosovo, which is part of modern Yugoslavia, was published in an American newspaper. It stated: 'Albania is almost entirely homogeneous, 97 percent, and was so at the time of its creation. Furthermore, the Albanians, descendants of the ancient Illyrians, are an indigenous people, and must have been in the Balkans since before recorded history. The Slavic peoples did not arrive in the Balkans until the seventh century AD.'[3] It was not spelled out why the late arrival of the Slavs should preclude them from living in the region, but the implications were clear.

Similarly, the Romanians claimed that they had a stronger right to inhabit the Transdanubian Basin than the other inhabitants of the region, and Ceausescu had himself proclaimed the most distinguished Romanian since the Dacian rulers. The East Germans began to honour all the outstanding Prussians, including Frederick the Great (not exactly a model of a socialist hero), while the Poles restored the royal castle in Warsaw and began to observe the millenia of various Christian anniversaries, including the conversion of the nation to Christianity (a feat only accomplished through the pressure of the Holy Roman Empire, headed by a German Emperor, and through the marriage of a Czech princess to a Polish prince, which clinched the matter). As these actions came from a regime which had claimed to eradicate religion for several decades, they might be called the apex of hypocrisy, except for one fact; that they enhanced and enforced latent chauvinistic attitudes among the population, and increased intolerance of their neighbours.

Patriotism has been called the last refuge of the scoundrel. To follow this, one might say that chauvinism is the symbol of failed government. The socialist governments which embrace chauvinism clearly state that the socialist experiment is at an end, because socialism's main tenet is international solidarity. Such ideology is a far cry from Eurocommunism which embraces the 'national road to socialism', but within the framework of international socialist ideology.

It is acknowledged that the East European governments' failures stem from the fact that they have not improved living standards for their people, and that this proves that socialism cannot be implemented. This is a spurious claim: socialism in Eastern Europe has not failed, because it has never been tried. And one of the main reasons that it has never been tried is partly connected with the inept, mediocre, self-serving leaders of the East European countries – though, of course, this is a simplistic explanation. Naturally, allowances must be made, because the leaders could only provide the kind of leadership of which they were capable. Such leadership centralised and enhanced state power, socialised certain sectors of the economy, and provided elements of the welfare state to some sections of the community. Though all these measures were important, they had little to do with either socialism, as expounded by Marx, or with Soviet power, as it was first understood after the Bolshevik Revolution.

As had been the case since 1945, the leadership had to come from the CPSU. When Mr Gorbachev came to power in the Soviet Union, he provided the first spark. Gorbachev is the first genuinely modern Soviet leader, yet one who has a concept of socialism which is much nearer to the original theory than those of his predecessors. Because of his conviction that the misapplication of the theory had retarded the development of the USSR and the Eastern Bloc, he began to encourage the leadership of the Bloc to update the theory and practice – a difficult task. One analyst summed it up in the following way:

> Mikhail Gorbachev is trying to shape those changes along the lines of his own policies in the Soviet Union. He prods his Eastern European cohorts towards economic reforms and reassures them of continued support. Moscow needs to revitalize these neighbouring economies to help its own, especially as markets for Soviet goods. But economic cures require political change - risky in the Soviet Union and riskier still for governments lacking nationalist legitimacy. Orthodox Eastern European parties have responded to Mr Gorbachev's call for reform with caution and with 'a nationalist approach to socialism'. This translates differently in each country.

In some cases, of course, the reforms were forced on the country by circumstances. General Jaruzelski, who, at sixty-three, was the youngest leader in the Bloc in 1987, had to introduce reforms in the wake of the Solidarity upheaval, and was continuing them in 1989. Hungary, led until 1988 by the very elderly Janos Kadar, and once the success story of the Bloc, had the largest foreign debt per capita. Living standards were falling and social tensions were growing. Kadar was forced to retire and nominate a younger successor to try to lead the country out of the impasse. Bulgaria has paid lip-service to reform, but has done little more than change its central management system slightly.

But these were countries whose leaders acknowledged that some change was needed. Mr Gorbachev's biggest problems were caused by those leaders who adamantly refused to reform and resisted change. Among them was Czechoslovakia, led until 1987 by the ossified Husak, who had been in charge of the country since the late 1960s. Husak was on the record as saying that reforms had led the country to the brink of disaster before and he did not intend to introduce any changes. His successor seems to have followed in his footsteps, and Czechoslovakia is still suffering from economic decay and political repression in 1989. Erich Honecker, East Germany's elderly leader, noted that his country had enjoyed economic success under his management, and therefore did not need to carry out reforms.

But perhaps the biggest difficulty, in political, if not in economic terms, was created by Romania. 'Rumania is virulently anti-reformist,' noted one observer:

> Nicolae Ceausescu, 69 and ailing, answers economic distress with more repression and austerity. Rumanians this week took to the streets in violent protest. They inquire plaintively about Soviet reforms. But when Mr Gorbachev came to explain them, Mr Ceausescu could only stare at his watch.[4]

Such national problems and personality divergences have existed in the Bloc for several decades, and were often encouraged, particularly after Stalin's death. But though they served to reassure the leaders of their power, and often appeased the population, always ready to play up to patriotic claims, they did little to advance the social and economic progress of their respective countries. The East German economic miracle owed much more to clever planners and technologists and to the hard-working population than to socialist ideology. Most other countries have probably regressed in real terms; sometimes due to the introduction of ill-considered mixed economy (as in Hungary); sometimes to petrification (as in Czechoslovakia). In other countries, disturbing revolts of a kind not experienced before have been in evidence. The best example of these is the Polish Solidarity movement; but there have been other examples of unrest.

Not all the difficulties in the Bloc have been caused by internal policies; the economic crisis which affected Western Europe in the 1970s, due to increased oil prices, has also had repercussions in Eastern Europe. But the policies of the elderly and often ailing leaders helped to exacerbate the situation. As the Soviet leadership needed to show some progress, particularly since Mikhail Gorbachev was testing his powers of persuasion, some things began to change, albeit very slowly.

Perestroika in the Eastern Bloc

On the seventieth anniversary of the Bolshevik Revolution, Mr Gorbachev made a long speech in which he outlined the future of socialism. The speech was not particularly well received in any country of the Socialist Bloc. The East German press devoted some space to Chinese affairs, alongside the text of the speech. But the Polish press saw it as a vindication of Jaruzelski's policy.

> Poland's reporting sought to award General Wojciech Jaruzelski . . . a principal supporting role in the cast of reformers surrounding Mr Gorbachev. General Jaruzelski was the first non-Soviet leader to address the Kremlin gathering after Mr Gorbachev and the first East bloc leader to meet the Soviet leader privately today. General Jaruzelski's speech, which was printed in full along with that of Mr Gorbachev, stressed the watershed character of the Moscow anniversary celebrations.

Jaruzelski even referred to the Soviet reforms as the 'Soviet springtime', which the author of the report considered was an unintended irony. While this is possible, it is well known that the Poles are expert at irony and black humour, and it is not improbable that the general knew very well what he was saying. However, what mattered most was the gist of Jaruzelski's speech, in which he made clear that 'Transformations reaching to the core are coming. They reflect the objective regularity of historical development. This is . . . a lasting and irreversible process.'[5]

While General Jaruzelski may have needed the reforms or a semblance of change more urgently than the leaders of the other Bloc countries, there is no doubt that change was inevitable – even if only a change of leadership, and not of the substance of government. But generational change alone will probably ensure that a change of substance will occur at a later stage. Some signs were already visible in 1987. The first leader to give up his post was Gustav Husak. He had attained his post almost twenty years earlier, in order to stop the kind of reforms which Gorbachev was advocating in the 1980s. In mid-December 1987, it was announced that Husak was stepping down as head of the party. But he did not step down in favour of a young reformer. He was replaced by Milos Jakes, a member of the Presidium. 'Mr Jakes, who is 65 years old, has generally been forecast as the successor to Mr Husak . . .,' stated one observer. Though Jakes' accession did not presage any radical change in the country, Mr Gorbachev sent him a telegram, urging him to begin the 'restructuring of the economy', and the 'democratization of public and political life'.[6]

Hungary was the next country to opt for change. As noted in a previous chapter, Kadar had to go and make way for a young pragmatist, though he did so with regret. But more substantive changes were in the offing. 'On Tuesday, the Hungarian parliament elected a biologist, Bruno Straub, as the country's first non-Communist president since World War II. Although the position is largely ceremonial, the move is viewed as a gesture towards social forces outside the Communist Party.'

However, in other countries, resistance continued. In Czechoslovakia, 'Mr Jakes stressed a need for enhancing the party's role as the leading force in society'. In Germany, Mr Honecker stated: 'Obviously it is a question of wanting to break up a certain encrustation of economic life in order to achieve a socioeconomic acceleration.' He supported the effort, but maintained that it had to be carried out in an entirely different manner in each country. 'We intend to continue the previously proved way,' he added.[7]

But little has been done to remove the main obstacles to progress. While many state agencies have been dismantled, the apparatus remains in place. And the nature of the system may not allow any more relaxation, because it is feared that if one brick is removed, the whole edifice may collapse. Modernisation would require much more than a relaxation of some controls. As one writer commented:

> Mikhail Gorbachev has decided that totalitarian control is not compatible with modernization and is not necessary to the continued political control by the Communist Party. He is surely right about the former proposition. Time will tell whether the monopoly of political power can be maintained if control over the economy and culture is relinquished. Is it possible that we are watching the early stage of an evolution of totalitarian states into authoritarian regimes?[8]

One may add that this commentator's definition of authoritarian and totalitarian regimes may not be that of other analysts. However, even that commentator admits that a change of substance may be about to occur. One must now look at future prospects.

Notes

1.   'East-Bloc emancipation: the search for a model', *International Herald Tribune*, 13 December 1988.

2. The situation in Poland has been discussed in Olga A. Narkiewicz, 'Polish or socialist?', *Universities Quarterly*, September 1965, p. 346.

3. See letter from Donald Leka, *New York Times*, 25 November 1987.

4. 'Heeding Eastern Europe now', *New York Times*, 23 November 1987.

5. 'East Bloc divided on speech', *New York Times*, 4 November 1987.

6. Jakes was born in 1922, in a provincial Bohemian town and became an electrician. He joined the party in 1945 and became the head of the Communist youth organisation in 1955, after which followed a period of study at the party school in Moscow. He became a member of the Secretariat in 1977, and of the Presidium in 1981. Though ideologically orthodox, he is said to be a mild supporter of a programme of economic changes. Vaclav Havel, a member of the Charter 77 organisation, said that Jakes would continue the same anti-reformist policies as Husak. But he added that he might pave the way for a new leader who would be reformist. This would prove necessary in view of the fact that the Czechoslovak economy was suffering in the late 1980s: 'the industrial sector, which before World War II was among Europe's leading manufacturing centers, is in decay, with low growth rates and stagnation setting in'. See 'Husak steps down as Prague leader', *New York Times*, 13 December 1987.

7. 'East Europe's eyes are on Moscow', *International Herald Tribune*, 2–3 July 1988.

8. Jeane Kirkpatrick, 'Demise of the totalitarian state in the Soviet Bloc?', *International Herald Tribune*, 28 October 1988.

9

Prospects for the future

The East European toboggan

The combined results of President Gorbachev's policies and the growing economic and political difficulties in the Soviet Union and the Socialist Bloc resulted in attention being focused on the possibility of the dissolution of the Bloc. Towards the end of the 1980s many Western analysts began to believe that the end of socialism was nearing, and that the socialist states would soon turn towards capitalism. While many welcomed the changes as proof that socialism was bankrupt, there were also some warning voices. The long period of Cold War, followed by many years of less virulent hostility, but of hostility nevertheless, did not prepare anyone for a lowering of tensions, nor for a possible disappearance of two opposing blocs.

One journalist noted that 'foreign policy experts from London to Rome are asking whether the rigid ideological division of Europe may be giving way to a much more fluid, fragmented and potentially more dangerous arrangement'. An opinion arose which thought that the feverish situation in the Bloc as reforms were being implemented (or, in some cases, not being implemented), and the lack of any Western policy in place in this situation, could prove dangerous. It was acknowledged that 'only West Germany has a fully developed strategy for Eastern Europe – one that puts a premium on encouraging evolutionary change and avoiding upheaval'.[1]

Many senior politicians shared these fears. One of President Mitterrand's senior advisers said in Paris that 'Eastern Europe could become a zone of instability and risk. I think they are all launched on a toboggan and they do not know where they are going to end up.'[2] Such worries were partly due to traditional attitudes: Europe had been divided into two camps since 1945 and the West found it difficult to imagine a different order of things. Most politicians and analysts could not remember the pre-war Europe of small nations, and while the rearrangement into two major blocs was condemned on ideological grounds, in some ways it suited not only the East, but also the West. Even bigger worries were voiced in Western capitals. Perhaps Gorbachev's policies would destabilise the Bloc? Perhaps the reforms which were being carried out in some countries would lead to upheavals comparable to the Hungarian revolution of 1956? Perhaps the Russians would be forced to react to such disorders in an armed fashion? Or, perhaps – and this was the biggest fear – the continued unrest in Eastern Europe and lack of economic success in the USSR would bring about the downfall of Gorbachev and the new policy of peaceful co-existence which he had instituted.

But the fears applied not only to the events which might happen in the Socialist Bloc. The West was alarmed about the stability of NATO, in the case of West Germany being drawn further to the East by the growing interest in trade exhibited in the Eastern Bloc. There was a further problem, even if it was barely mentioned. 'The debate about Eastern Europe is ultimately a camouflaged debate about the destiny of Germany, where the East–West ideological fault line runs through a nation sundered by World War II.'[3] Dreams of unification, of a thriving trade relationship with Eastern Europe, and still quiescent, but nevertheless strong, sentiments about the German Eastern territories lost to Poland, all led to the development of West Germany's 'special relationship' with the East European countries. The French were particularly worried about such developments. France's weaker economy and smaller population could not stand up to the new power of West Germany. 'There is a feeling that while we were playing politics in the 1980s, denouncing Jaruzelski or whatever, the Germans were making money and conquering markets', said a French analyst, commenting further that France was left without a policy and without new markets. Equally annoyed were some American politicians, though for different reasons. They felt that the West Germans were exporting strategic materials to the East, and making money, while US manufacturers were forbidden to do the same by Federal regulations. In the West there was even talk of 'the Germanization of Western Europe's Ostpolitik'; an ironic term in view of the fact that west of Germany there had been no policy towards Western Europe, except that outlined in Washington.[4]

In view of such a climate of opinion, and the almost alarmist views expressed in Western circles, President Gorbachev adopted a very subtle policy, one which confused the West even more, though it is probable that it was not done with this aim in view. It is more likely that Gorbachev was only concerned with pacifying Eastern Europe without upsetting Western Europe and the United States. Coincidentally, he was trying to improve the Soviet economic position by allowing the Socialist Bloc countries to obtain Western loans, thus relieving the Soviet Union of the burden, and making the Bloc less dependent on Soviet help. The policy was not completely new; it had been followed during the first period of détente, but Gorbachev and his advisers refined it to the point which left the West wondering about its final outcome.

Some analysts even concluded that Soviet totalitarian control was at an end. These moves, one of them suggested, could even mean that Gorbachev was ready to abandon the efforts at total control, because he has decided that 'totalitarian control is not compatible with modernization and is not necessary to continued political control by the Communist Party. . . . Is it possible that we are watching the early stages of an evolution of totalitarian states into authoritarian regimes?' one asked.[5]

If the West was puzzled and expected either a series of revolutions or the dissolution of the Soviet state, followed by a dissolution of the Bloc, the East fared even worse. Gorbachev had appointed Vadim Medvedev to the chief ideological post, to replace the conservative Yegor Ligachev. It was believed that Medvedev constructed the new policy towards Eastern Europe, 'which emphasizes the relative freedom of Communist-ruled states to pursue their own "paths to socialism" as well as closer economic integration of the bloc'.[6] It might have been expected that, under the pressure of the new Gorbachev team, the East European leaders would resign *en masse*.

It turned out, however, that the situation was more complex.

The leaders who resigned were those in Hungary and Poland, countries which were already faithfully implementing Gorbachev's new policies. Leaders of the other countries paid lip-service to the reforms, but asserted either that such reforms had already been carried out in their own countries, or that they were unnecessary. Even in countries where the old leader resigned, as happened in Czechoslovakia, he resigned in favour of a follower of the old policy of repression. Thus, Gorbachev's policy of supporting the 'national road to socialism', left some countries unreformed, while others attempted to reform under their own steam.

It is problematic whether Gorbachev had calculated this policy as an exercise in freedom and democracy. But, whatever the case, it was a propitious moment from the Soviet point of view, for it was irrelevant what policies and what leaders were in place in the Socialist Bloc at this point in time, provided they did not demand further substantial financial help from the Soviet Union. While the Soviet Union was quite capable of providing such help had it wanted to, Gorbachev had long ago decided that Soviet internal reforms were much more important than attending to the well-being of the allies. Therefore, the East European leaders were invited to apply for help to the West. In the West, the Germans (particularly the German banks) were willing. The French expressed an interest and provided some small loans. But it was on the United States that the most indebted states, Poland and Hungary, had counted.

At this moment, another leader appeared on the scene. For several decades the American presidents had designated themselves as 'leaders of the Free World'. When George Bush became president, he coveted the title as much as earlier presidents. His internal problems made it even more imperative that he should score success abroad. He therefore planned an East European tour to compensate for his lack of success at home. After some thought, a visit to Poland and Hungary was arranged for the president in early July 1989. He went there for 'the photo opportunity', as one journalist put it. 'The President expected to cut a superb dash in the East. In Poland and Hungary, tumultuous crowds would greet him as a beacon of freedom and a symbol of hope.' However, Bush's problem, that of being caught between the popularity of Ronald Reagan and that of Mikhail Gorbachev, was not solved in Eastern Europe. The crowds were reported to be sparse and quiet.

There were no interviews with the local population. Bush's difficulties, it appears, were not caused by his lack of charisma. Rather, they were caused by the fact that he was not bringing any gifts.[7]

One Western observer noted sarcastically:

As the world's biggest debtor nation, the US has at last begun to accept that it is simply too poor to undertake the kind of foreign policy it would prefer. George Bush has just spent four days in Poland and in Hungary hoping that the symbolism of his presence could make up for his empty pocket.

He added, 'Somehow, the irony of this trip has escaped the travelling White House'. For, he commented, if capitalism had won over socialism, where was the money to prove it?[8] Not only did Bush not offer money, but his entourage offended the East Europeans. John Sununu, Bush's chief of staff, compared a cash hand-out to Poland to 'putting a child into a candy store'.[9] It may not be surprising that the Americans were thus prepared to wound their staunch Eastern admirers for want of money. What may have surprised the Poles, however, was that they were suddenly left in a kind of limbo. Unable to get aid from the Soviet Union or the United States, the far-seeing General Jaruzelski reacted swiftly by resigning office. He was probably the only East European leader to appreciate the complexity of the dilemma: powerless to disband socialism, and too poor to embrace capitalism, Poland simply had nowhere to go. The second country Bush visited, Hungary, was careful not to press for money. The Hungarians smiled bravely and assured Bush that money would be useful, but was not essential. But it must be noted that throughout the summer of 1989, the Hungarian leadership was in turmoil, and the confusion did not diminish after the president's visit.

As a result, a combination of new Soviet policies and America's inability to help left Eastern Europe or, at least, the reforming countries, out in the cold. This allowed the conservatives in the Bloc to smile smugly and maintain that hardline policies had been right, because the low debt of their countries did not put them at the mercy of either the Soviet Union or the United States. Towards the end of the summer of 1989, it appeared that the leaders of the reformist countries were penalised, while the hardliners were winning.

The dilemma of reformed leaderships

The reason that the reformed leaderships, rather than the conservatives, had problems, lay embedded in the history of the Socialist Bloc. Its more profound causes could be found in the history of the Soviet Union itself. At the outset of its existence, the Soviet Union was not a country committed to status quo. On the contrary, it carried the most revolutionary message in modern times, even more revolutionary than that of the French Revolution. However, due partly to external pressures, and partly to internal inflexibility, the country gradually petrified in its practice. The apex of this petrification occurred in the latter years of Leonid Brezhnev's leadership and became known as *immobilisme*.

It has been noted in the previous chapters that the East European leaderships were for many decades forced into the same pattern of government as the Soviet Union, and, as the Soviet Union became increasingly immobile, so did the East European governments. When the Soviet Union regained impetus under the leadership of Mikhail Gorbachev and his new team of technocrats, East European governments were pressed to introduce substantial reforms. However, the nature of such reforms has to be carefully examined. It has been pointed out that Gorbachev's reforms, known as *perestroika*, were forced by the economic standstill in the Soviet Union, and not by the realisation that the political system was inadequate.[10] Consequently, the leaders of those countries whose economies were not in immediate danger, or those who were outside the framework of co-operation within the Bloc, decided that there was no need to reform their countries. The majority of the countries in the Bloc belonged to this category, which comprised East Germany, Bulgaria, Czechoslovakia and Romania. It fell to the leaders of the most volatile countries, Poland and Hungary, to implement the reforms. And, as Poland and Hungary had already undergone several revolutions (some of them bloody), they may have been less than willing to implement a process of basic reconstruction. However, the pressures these governments encountered, both from their own populations and from the Soviet Union, made it imperative that they should carry out reforms. They set about the task with some hesitation and the results were mixed.

Previously, Hungary had carried out substantial economic reforms under the leadership of Janos Kadar. These resulted in short-term prosperity, but produced high inflation in the long run, as well as some unemployment. As a result of these measures, Hungary had the dubious distinction of having the highest per capita debt in the Bloc, and no means to repay it. In the late 1980s, the country was forced to submit to the discipline of international banks, and had to restrict consumption and increase prices. This medicine was so unpalatable that the Communist leadership was inclined to relinquish its leading role and pass the reins of power to non-Communists. Measures which might have been introduced in 1956, but were not, because of Soviet intervention, were suddenly deemed essential thirty years later.

But before the change-over was made, a ritual had to be carried out. The leader of the 1956 uprising, Imre Nagy, was re-buried in the spring of 1989. It was reported that 'The presumed remains of former Prime Minister Imre Nagy had been exhumed from an unmarked grave with the cooperation of the Communist government that executed him after the 1956 Hungarian uprising.'[11] The remains from the unmarked grave may or may not have been those of Imre Nagy. In fact, Hungary was reinterring its own myth: the myth of independence and capitalist economy. Unfortunately, the years of dependence on the Soviet Union's help did not prepare either the government or the nation for the hardships which accompanied an independent status.

The precarious nature of the Hungarian economy was soon shown in the fact that the new president-in-waiting (as he has been called) missed a session of the Hungarian parliament, in order to have a private meeting with President Bush, then on a brief visit to Hungary.[12] The future presidential candidate, Pozsgay, had already managed to oust Karoly Grosz, and was nominated by the party. Possibly in anticipation of American loans, he immediately announced that, when free elections would be held in twelve months' time, the party would give up power if it was defeated at the polls. His promises were taken with a pinch of salt. One correspondent commented: 'If that happens, he should not be affected too badly. By then he should be a national, non-party, very powerful president.'[13]

It is a matter for conjecture on whose advice the change-over was made, and who was the gainer. The Soviet Union had clearly gained, because it no longer felt obliged to extend economic aid to Hungary. The United States had gained, because it could point to the victory of the capitalist over the Communist system. A minor gainer was Mr Pozsgay, who gained a powerful post, though he may yet live to regret it. But the overall losers were the Hungarians. To make them feel better about the future, they were given a few carrots. The man who was said to have been responsible for the arrest and interrogation of Imre Nagy in 1956, Sandor Rajnai, resigned from the Central Committee of the party and announced his resignation as ambassador to the Soviet Union on 2 June 1989.[14] The ritual purge of past wrong-doers was accompanied by a ritual call within the party for 'neutrality guaranteed by the two superpowers' and for a transition to a multi-party system.[15]

There was one last ritual which had to be gone through: the saviour of the nation and the executor of Imre Nagy had to be buried. Almost symbolically, Janos Kadar died in early July 1989, little more than a year after his resignation from leadership. The last few years had not been easy, for it was forgotten that for all his crimes against the revolutionaries, he had given Hungary a dose of stability and prosperity which other countries in the Bloc envied. He was condemned for having stayed on for too long: 'At the end, he was unable to let go. His final speech to political activists in May 1988, was tearful, rambling and pathetic. He had become a political monument and had outstayed his welcome.'[16] On 14 July, Kadar was buried in a state funeral. Two days later, the prime minister and other leading politicians paid tribute to the man Kadar had had executed, Imre Nagy.

But the burying and re-burying of bodies did not solve the problems of government and economy. As early as the end of June, the opinion was that Hungary was in a state of chaos. 'Nobody in Budapest can answer the question "Who is the boss?" as government spokesmen explain the new arrangements for a collectived party praesidium', commented one observer. The commentary consoled itself with the thought that Hungary may enjoy liberation from the decades of one-man rule, with which it had been encumbered. But the changes in the party and government posts which occurred so suddenly may not work out well: 'none of this guarantees a trouble-free road to reform. It is always a tricky business tampering with entrenched party bureaucracies' it was concluded.[17]

A few weeks later a Hungarian who had lived abroad for several decades described the chaotic state of affairs in the country by saying that the only good government is a scared government. But judging by his account, there was no government to speak of in Hungary. President Gorbachev's statement that 'the Soviet army would not interfere again in Hungarian politics paralyzed Hungary's security police and broke the Communist Party's resistance to change'. He further qualified his statement by saying that 'Moral amnesia, equal sorrow for traitors and patriots, executioners and their innocent victims – this is how peaceful change is proceeding in Hungary'.[18] An objective observer might conclude that such a state of affairs seems more reminiscent of chaos than of amnesia. But this was only to be expected: the nation, dependent on many foreign powers over centuries, had suddenly lost its direction, having been deprived of Soviet tutelage and a strong leader.

It could be argued that the party had lost and the nation had won. But is this really the case? Hungary's choices are few. It may feel that it belongs to the West through its culture, but its insolvent state makes it an unlikely member of the prosperous West European organisations. On the other hand, the Soviet Union has distanced itself from Hungarian affairs, aware of its manifold problems. Hungary has few friends in the Balkan peninsula and is feuding with Romania. Though it has extended feelers towards Austria, the one country with which it has had historical links in the nineteenth century, Austria has resolutely turned down any idea of re-creating the Austro-Hungarian Empire in a new form. Hungary's old friendship with Poland would be useful, if Poland had something to offer. But Poland's economic and political problems are even more difficult than those of Hungary. Indebted and bewildered, the country stands alone, facing calls to repay its debts and to 'democratise'. Few people, both inside and outside Hungary, have any clear idea of how such democratisation could begin. But the one factor which could help Hungary to regain its footing, massive financial help, is being denied; partly because of pressure by the banks, and partly because of the American deficit. If this state of affairs continues, Hungary will slide into complete chaos; such an outcome will be in no one's interests.

If Hungary had led the way towards economic liberalisation, only to find that it could not succeed without political liberalisation, the other restless country in the Bloc, Poland, followed a different path. Poland's economy had been in trouble for several decades, and periodic disturbances followed as a result. But, in retrospect, it can be concluded that the Poles viewed the economic aspect of the country's problems as a marginal – though vital – one. What the nation was really asking for, through the medium of food riots, was a greater degree of independence from the Soviet Union, and the right to make its own decisions.

The emergence of Solidarity at the beginning of the 1980s brought these two strands, the economic and the political, together, and brought forward a leader in the nation's own image. Lech Walesa, the founder of Solidarity, was articulate, outspoken, religious, anti-Communist and insubordinate. He exemplified all the national characteristics which had been enhanced since the end of the Second World War, and fitted the mood of the country. However, his personality was more than matched by the personality of the man who quelled the Solidarity disturbances. General Jaruzelski had a mind of his own, was a quick decision-maker, and could be considered Walesa's antithesis. Jaruzelski stood for all the values which Walesa despised, but did so in a particularly Polish way, which made him more than a match for the unruly free trade union leader.

Had Mikhail Gorbachev not come to power soon after the suppression of Solidarity, one could have envisaged further repressive measures against Poland, and possibly even a Warsaw Pact invasion. But Gorbachev's policy of non-interference, coupled with his close ties with Jaruzelski, ensured that this did not happen. Instead, after a long period of in-fighting, strikes, and a further collapse of the economy, a compromise was arranged between the warring parties. Some signs of this compromise were emerging in late 1988, but it was not until early 1989 that the shape of things to come began to emerge.

As far as can be assessed, the Hungarian solution was applied in Poland, though with some modifications. The country was to be allowed some political freedom, but would have to pay for it with economic misery. It was noted that 'As Poland prepares to break ground for its new program of democratization, General Wojciech Jaruzelski is seeking to reshape his image from that of a tough party leader . . . to that of a patriotic statesman who can act as a guarantor of stability.'[19] In the wake of the government's decision to re-legalise Solidarity and to call new elections, Jaruzelski kept his counsel and did not join in any discussions with the union. He was said to have been bitter and melancholy as the measures which he had instituted in 1981 were being reversed one by one. However, he did not protest, probably realising that a permanent state of marital law, or a covert civil war could not continue forever.

Nevertheless, even in his retreat, there were prizes to be won. General Jaruzelski was 'poised to become the first Polish Communist leader to survive the recurring cycle of stagnation, crisis and upheaval that has haunted Communist Party rule, and his supporters say they believe he could yet reshape his political image and place in Polish history'.[20] His role was to become an elder statesman, who would watch over the democratisation of the country from his new position as a powerful president. Many hopes were placed on this role. There was little but praise for his personal virtues, despite lack of enthusiasm from Solidarity leaders. 'Jaruzelski has always been less of a Communist than a Polish patriot,' commented one party collaborator. A party journalist concurred: 'Maybe he was too cautious. . . . But the end result was that he civilized the party and civilized the opposition and made it possible for them to work together.' It was admitted that for all his failures, and the procrastination in removing the martial law, he had proved more adept than his predecessors in instituting change. 'While Edward Gierek and Wladyslaw Gomulka stubbornly refused to change course, General Jaruzelski responded to the waves of strikes . . . by dismissing his prime minister . . . and bringing new, younger politicians into the party leadership.'[21]

These optimistic views were soon silenced, as the political situation slid into the – by then – normal round of warfare. As the new, semi-free elections approached in early June 1989, the polls forecast that 58.2 per cent of the votes would be cast for Solidarity candidates and 3.7 per cent for the party candidates.[22] This forecast proved only too accurate. The party lost the elections so badly that four weeks later General Jaruzelski announced that he would not stand as a presidential candidate, a post which, it was assumed, he would have won easily. Chaos appeared imminent in the party and the country, as Jaruzelski announced at the end of June that if he stood in the way of reconciliation, he would be ready to retire. 'When there is an obstacle to reconciliation, to uniting social forces, there is only one possible solution – even if that obstacle is Wojciech Jaruzelski,' he said. The comment was rather acid: 'This may seem remarkably self-effacing, but it can also be interpreted as a sign of pragmatism in a man who, as his critics have occasionally jibed, learnt during his Jesuit education, to make the means serve the end.'[23] In standing down, the general suggested a new candidate, a close associate of his, the minister of the interior, General Czeslaw Kiszczak.

The situation soon developed into a farce, but a farce which could have serious consequences for the country. Walesa came under increasing pressure to run for the presidency. He refused to do so, but intimated that Solidarity would be willing to construct a government, in return for which it would support a Communist president.[24] The situation became more complicated every day. President Bush was to arrive in Warsaw in early July, and had to be greeted by the head of state. Solidarity was split on the issue of the presidency and the new government. The party was split on the same issues, as well as on the issues of Solidarity. Western governments were pressing Solidarity to assume power; Western banks, always in favour of stability, were pressing Solidarity to allow Jaruzelski, in whom they had confidence, to continue in power. And to add to the confusion, the Soviet Union, on whose intervention everyone was counting, in order to be absolved from all blame, was turning a blind eye, and allowing the Poles a lot of leeway.

Poland has been accustomed to internal splits and to pressures from its big neighbours for many centuries. But this time they were contradictory and they came from too many directions. It was difficult to respond rationally. In the end, the less sophisticated Solidarity leaders were overcome by the Jesuit-trained General Jaruzelski. In mid-July, Walesa indicated that Solidarity would support Jaruzelski's candidacy for president, aware that the situation was getting desperate. 'Five weeks on from the election, none of the key questions of presidency, prime minister, or government have been solved.'[25]

Eventually Jaruzelski was voted in as president, but with the narrowest possible majority. The vote in the Sejm was 270 in favour, one more than he needed to be elected; 34 members abstained and 233 voted against him. Hardly ever had a future executive president obtained such a slim mandate. After the election, Jaruzelski said in his speech of acceptance that he wanted to be 'a president of reconciliation, a representative of all Poles. I will serve the nation. I will serve the fatherland, the one that has not perished, the one that is and will be,' thus alluding to the words of the Polish national anthem. However, the ceremony did not pass without bitterness. Bronislaw Geremek, the leader of parliamentary Solidarity, stated that the country would never forget Jaruzelski's role in imposing martial law.[26]

Nevertheless, the crisis was not over yet. Jaruzelski now asked General Kiszczak to form a government of broad coalition. After two weeks Kiszczak gave up the task and passed it on to the leader of the United Peasant Party, Roman Malinowski. In the meantime, Moscow was beginning to voice concern. It was reported that the 'Soviet Communist Party newspaper, *Pravda* accused Mr Walesa yesterday of provoking a crisis by refusing to join a Communist-led government'. Walesa responded on the following day by stating that the opposition would accept a deal which allowed the Communist Party to keep the defence and interior ministries. He told reporters: 'The most important ministries which are the base of the physical continuity of the state should stay in the hands of the Communist Party.' The way was opened for a coalition government of the majority: the opposition Solidarity, the centre UPP (United Peasant Party) and Democratic Party, and two ministers from the Communist Party. The parliamentary Solidarity passed a resolution asking Walesa to become prime minister, but he refused.[27]

Walesa had been in public life for nearly a decade. During this period he had travelled extensively, had received wide recognition, and appeared poised on the way to one of the highest offices in the land. His refusal to accept the post of prime minister at this stage might have been puzzling, except for one reason: he was aware of the financial situation of the country. Meeting in Paris in July 1989, Western leaders

> rejected calls for a substantial bail-out of Eastern Europe, but expressed support for Bush's modest package of proposals. These include $150m aid for Poland and Hungary, a commitment to reschedule the two countries' combined $57 billion foreign debt, and a suggestion that all Western aid to Eastern Europe be co-ordinated through one agency.

The leaders claimed that their proposals would reward those countries which have moved towards capitalism and encourage others to move in this way, too.[28] Warnings have been sounded out about this parsimonious attitude: 'Critics claim the West is missing an historic opportunity to reshape the map of Europe, and is risking an economic crisis which could push the reforming countries back to totalitarian communism or over the brink into anarchy,' said one analyst.[29]

There were warnings on the other side, too. Walesa was not thought a suitable person for the post. When he addressed a meeting in Gdansk, speaking at the monument to the shipyard workers who were killed in 1970, 'Lech Walesa made a typical wild declaration of optimism. "We want to be the America of Eastern Europe",' he declared. It was further noted that

> He is prone to exaggeration. Only a day earlier he had told an American television network that economic reform without substantial Western aid could lead to civil war. In front of Bush, he issued an even more apocalyptic warning: if the West did not help, it might have to watch another Tiananmen Square massacre, this time in Poland.[30]

In the end, the post was not offered to any outstanding Solidarity personalities, but to a middle-aged journalist, Tadeusz Mazowiecki.[31] Some disquiet was voiced about this appointment. Mazowiecki, a Catholic journalist, was little known in the country, and completely unknown outside the country. Moreover, his experience of government was non-existent. It was commented that 'With little experience in business, Mr Mazowiecki will face a serious test in doing something about the moribund economy. But the single most pointed criticism that Mr Mazowiecki faces . . . is grounded not in economics but in his links to the church.' It was even suggested that Mazowiecki's appointment was arranged in a series of meetings between General Jaruzelski, the Polish Cardinal Glemp and the Soviet ambassador to Warsaw. It was also pointed out that it was the first time since the eighteenth century that the Polish Primate had met with a Russian envoy in Warsaw.[32]

In a terse statement on 19 August, the president announced that he had asked Mazowiecki, 'a long-time Catholic activist' to take the post of prime minister.[33] Almost immediately, the Central Committee of the party met in an emergency session and demanded two more ministerial posts than had been agreed previously: those of the foreign and finance ministers.[34] Eventually, after much wrangling, a coalition goverment was agreed in the first half of September. It gave nine seats to Solidarity, six to centre parties and four, those of the interior, defence, transport and foreign trade, to the Communist Party.

Some commentators noted that the installation of a non-Communist government in a socialist country was a dangerous experiment, but one which was unavoidable. One stated that 'Unmanageable change in Poland is the last thing reform Communists need now. . . . A Solidarity-led government is a *desperate gamble* to manage the accelerating change.'[35] The government's first task will be to set the economy of the country on the right course. It remains to be seen whether the non-Communists will succeed any better than the Communists in this onerous task.

Voting with their feet

While such momentous changes were on the way in Poland and Hungary, little seemed to be happening in other countries of the Bloc. But their leaders were getting older and more tired. Erich Honecker had been taken ill in the summer and had to undergo gall bladder surgery. This did not prove successful. Some sources reported that 'doctors had to halt the operation because the condition of the organ had deteriorated. . . . East Germany denied the reports about Mr Honecker, 77. A Foreign Ministry spokesman in East Berlin said he was "progressing toward recovery".'[36]

But the East Germans were tired of waiting for Honecker to retire or die. They took to escape to show their disgust with the petrification of their country under his continuing leadership. Thousands of East German citizens took the road to West Germany, once Hungary had eliminated border controls with Austria. The exodus took West Germany by surprise, since the standards of living in East Germany had been the highest in the Bloc, and the migration did not seem to be the result of economic hardship. Some commentators put it down to lack of Gorbachev-style reforms. Others mentioned political and economic stagnation. There were even those who believed that Honecker was allowing emigration in order to eliminate the discontented citizens from the country. A West German official commented that 'He really seems to think that if he lets the discontented ones leave, the country will become more stable.'[37]

Others thought differently. It was now believed that Honecker may be suffering from cancer, and that a power struggle was going on in the Politburo. But there were deeper concerns as well. Whoever replaced Honecker would have to come to grips with the possibility of the re-unification of two Germanies; a scenario that Honecker would not contemplate. 'President Mikhail Gorbachev has, perhaps unwittingly, breathed life into the long somnolent "German question", his frequent calls for "a common European home" seem to suggest the possibility of a single German state.'[38] The reminders that Germany is one nation do come mostly from West German politicians. But it cannot be forgotten that in the fairly recent past, the East German politicians had similar goals, though they would have a united socialist Germany, not a capitalist one.

Honecker had kept the reins of power for so long and so tightly that no strong-minded leader had emerged in East Germany to carry out such unification. Nor is West Germany likely to produce a leader, sufficiently indifferent to Western opinion, who would be willing to unify the country. François Mauriac's saying that 'I love Germany so much I am glad there are two of them' has sunk into West German mythology. The West is not happy about the scenario of an East-leaning Germany and its effects on NATO and the European Common Market. But, for reasons which may be grounded in economics, or traditional politics, the Soviet leadership seems to contemplate just such a scenario. Mikhail Gorbachev's references to a 'common European home' may not be as naïve as has been believed. For, in the meantime, someone has already constructed a plan for re-unification, and has floated a trial balloon.

> The scenario for reunification is complicated. It could run like this: Mikhail Gorbachev proposes a radical breakthrough in the Vienna arms talks, halving the number of Soviet troops in Eastern Europe in return for similar American measures; then a five-year timetable for withdrawal of all forces in Europe to within national frontiers, a Russian retreat matched by an American pull-out and disbandment of the British Army of the Rhine.

Honecker dies and is replaced by a temporary leader who refuses to reform. The exodus of East Germans continues. Finally, some relaxation is allowed in East Germany; Poland and Hungary become associate members of the European Community. Moscow winds up the Warsaw Pact and West Germany leaves NATO. A referendum in both Germanies is in favour of re-unification. Berlin is reunited as the federal capital, and the EEC drops its single market in favour of free trade agreements with the Soviet Union and other socialist countries. 'It sounds almost as far-fetched as the situation in Eastern Europe today would have done when Leonid Brezhnev was in the Kremlin – and that was only seven years ago.'[39]

The unified Germany would be a new state and might not go down too well in Bonn – after all, Bonn is nearer to France than Berlin, and West German politicians have a cultural yearning to be close to the French (not really reciprocated by the French, it must be admitted). But Honecker's death, probably not far off, and the lack of a credible successor, combined with the strong leadership of Mikhail Gorbachev, might yet accomplish this feat. From the Soviet and American points of view, the saving on troop expenditure might warrant the risk of a united and possibly aggressive new Germany. But what of the Europeans? Will Nazi Germany's victims, Poland and Czechoslovakia, view such developments with indifference? Even if the main combatants, France and Britain, were to agree to a united Germany, it cannot be denied that the map of Europe, as it has been known since the end of the Second World War, would be completely changed. It may yet be that the world will long for the days of stability, as exemplified by Honecker and Husak.

Already, the Bush Administration is showing signs of alarm, and the deputy secretary of state is on record as saying that the Cold War was characterised by a stable set of relationships between the great powers, whereas the rising trend of multilateral relations may prove to be 'too destabilizing to be sustained'.[40] And the Eastern Europeans may not be any happier. At a recent conference, the participants viewed the prospect of the collapse of the Socialist Bloc, and most particularly, the phasing out of the East German regime, as highly alarming. The changes in the Bloc were too rapid to be beneficial, it was opined. East Germany was not scheduled to liberalise yet, but the feat has been accomplished through the desertion of her citizens. In Poland and Hungary, the Communists were out of power; will the other countries of the Bloc follow suit? This seems to be only a matter of time. In that case, will the Warsaw Pact collapse as well, and if so, what will be the consequences?

On one thing, all participants agreed: 'There is no way of re-forming totalitarian systems in peacemeal fashion. . . . The fall of the world's last empire is unlikely to prove an exception. "I have found from our discussions that neither you in the West nor we in the East know what to do," said a Pole.'[41] It may be that Gorbachev will survive the partial dismantling of the Soviet Bloc, and the other leaders in the Bloc will disappear of natural causes. But one must admit that there is one leader who has seen the writing on the wall: the great survivor, President Jaruzelski. In the first interview granted a television network since accession to the presidency, Jaruzelski stated unequivocally that though Communism is a great historical idea, it is Utopian. Though Communist revolutions have improved the lot of millions of people, the distortions of Stalinism have eroded this idea. Because of Stalinsim, it was found that a monopolistic government is ineffective, and authentic democracy is necessary for progress.[42] It is a view the General very likely shares with President Gorbachev.

Future historians will decide whether bad leadership led to the collapse of the Socialist Bloc (assuming that it does collapse), or whether Marx's ideas are impossible to carry out in practice. All one can state at this stage is that the Socialist Bloc has not enjoyed good leadership in all the decades of its existence. Whether this is the function of the system, or of other difficulties, is impossible to establish at the moment.

Notes

1. 'An East European toboggan: as Moscow's grip eases, the balance of power skids', *International Herald Tribune*, 27 February 1989.
2. *Ibid.*
3. *Ibid.*
4. *Ibid.*
5. Jeane Kirkpatrick, 'Demise of the totalitarian state in the Soviet Bloc?', *International Herald Tribune*, 28 October 1988.
6. 'East Europe awaits Soviet shock waves', *International Herald Tribune*, 4 October 1988.
7. 'The hollow Eastern European campaign', *The Observer*, 16 July 1989.
8. Martin Walker, 'Strapped for cash, stumped for solutions', *The Guardian*, 12 July 1989.
9. 'The hollow Eastern European campaign.'

10. See Padma Desai, *Perestroika in Perspective*, Princeton University Press, 1989, and Anders Aslund, *Gorbachev's Struggle for Economic Reform*, Cornell University Press, 1989.

11. 'Hungary moves to rebury leader of 1956 uprising', *International Herald Tribune*, 31 March 1989.

12. 'Pozsgay skips parliament to attend private talks', *The Guardian*, 13 May 1989.

13. *Ibid.*

14. 'Responsable de l'interrogatoire de Nagy l'ambassadeur de Hongrie a Moscou demissionne', *Le Monde*, 4–5 June 1989.

15. 'Hungary party radicals unite', *International Herald Tribune*, 23 May 1989.

16. 'The satrap who lived to become a patriot again', *The Guardian*, 7 July 1989.

17. 'Hungary's answer', *The Guardian*, 27 June 1989.

18. 'Running scared – Hungary's Communist regime', *The Globe and Mail*, Toronto, 3 August 1989.

19. 'Jaruzelski seeks image shift: tough party boss to statesman', *International Herald Tribune*, 21 March 1989.

20. *Ibid.*

21. *Ibid.*

22. 'Le pouvoir craint une victoire ecrasante de l'opposition', *Le Monde*, 4–5 June 1989. Figures from a poll by *Gazeta Wyborcza*, a Solidarity newspaper.

23. 'Jaruzelski set to hand over reins of power', *The Sunday Times*, 2 July 1989.

24. 'Solidarity contemplates bid to govern Poland', *The Guardian*, 3 July 1989.

25. 'Walesa boosts Solidarity backing for Jaruzelski', *The Guardian*, 15 July 1989.

26. 'Jaruzelski voted in as president', *The Guardian*, 20 July 1989.

27. 'Polish PM abandons coalition attempts', *The Globe and Mail*, 15 August 1989; 'Solidarity flexible on joining coalition', *The Globe and Mail*, 16 August 1989; 'Walesa endorsed for PM by Solidarity legislators', *The Globe and Mail*, 17 August 1989.

28. 'A fistful of dollars', *The Sunday Times*, 16 July 1989.

29. *Ibid.*

30. *Ibid.*

31. The 62-year-old Mazowiecki had trained as a lawyer, but was soon attracted to journalism. He edited a Catholic newspaper in Wroclaw, and became a leading member of the Catholic Pax group, which was thought by some to be close to government circles. He emerged in the 1980s as a moving force in the Solidarity organisation, and later became a chief negotiator between Solidarity and the goverment. See, 'A Catholic at the helm', *The New York Times*, 19 August 1989.

32. *Ibid.*

33. See 'Text of Polish statement', *The New York Times*, 20 August 1989.

34. 'Polish Communists threaten to withhold support for new coalition', *The Globe and Mail*, 24 August 1989.

35. 'Poland's roller coaster ride to reform', *The Globe and Mail*, 21 August 1989; from an editorial article in *The New York Times*; emphasis added.

36. 'East German leader's surgery reported halted', *Globe and Mail*, 31 August 1989.

37. 'Breaching the Wall', *Time Magazine*, 11 September 1989.

38. *Ibid.*

39. 'One nation, one Germany', *The Vancouver Sun*, 16 September 1989.

40. 'A bizarre nostalgia for the Cold War', *New York Times*, 19 September 1989.

41. 'Soviet change: a vast unknown', *The Vancouver Sun*, 20 September 1989.

42. 'Interview with President Jaruzelski', Public Broadcasting Corporation, The MacNeil/Lehrer News Hour, 18 September 1989.

Select bibliography

Bradley, J.F.N., *Politics in Czechoslovakia, 1945–1971*, Washington DC: University Press of America, 1981.

Bromke, Adam, 'Poland under Gierek: A new political style', *Problems of Communism*, September–October 1972.

Brown, J.F., *Bulgaria under Communist Rule*, New York; Praeger, 1970.

Burks, R.V., 'Romania and a theory of progress', *Problems of Communism*, May–June 1972.

Claudin, F., *The Communist Movement from Comintern to Cominform*, Harmondsworth: Penguin, 1975.

Conquest, R., *The Great Terror* (rev. edn), Harmondsworth: Penguin, 1971.

Croan, Melvin, 'Ostpolitik–Westpolitik', *Problems of Communism*, May–June 1973.

Deutscher, I., *Stalin: A political biography,* London: Oxford University Press, 1961.

Dziewanowski, M.K., *Communist Party of Poland*, Harvard: Harvard University Press, 1956.

Farlow, Robert A., 'Romanian foreign policy: a case of partial alignment', *Problems of Communism*, November–December 1971.

Fejto, F., *Portrait d'Imre Nagy: Un communiste qui a choisi le peuple*, Paris: Plon, 1957.

Fejto, F., *A History of the People's Democracies* (2nd edn), Harmondsworth: Penguin, 1974.

Fischer, Mary Ellen, 'Idol or leader? The origins and the future of the Ceausescu cult', in Nelson, D.N. (ed.) *Romania in the 1980s*, Boulder, Co.: Westview Press, 1981.

Johnson, A. Ross, 'Poland: end of an era?', *Problems of Communism*, January–February 1970.

Kovrig, B., *Communism in Hungary from Kun to Kadar*, Oxford: Clio Press, 1979.

Kto jest Kim w Polsce, 1984.

Kusin, V.V., 'Gorbachev and Eastern Europe', *Problems of Communism*, January–February 1986.

Larrabee, S., 'Bulgaria's politics of conformity', *Problems of Communism*, July–August 1972.

Lewytzkyj, B. and Stroynowski, J., *Who's Who in Socialist Countries*, New York and Munich: K.G. Saur Publishing Inc., 1978.

Liddell Hart, B.H., *History of the Second World War*, London: Pan Books, 1973.

Lippmann, Heinz, 'The limits of reform Communism', *Problems of Communism*, May–June 1970.

Lippmann, Heinz, *Honecker and the New Politics of Europe*, (trans. from German), New York: Macmillan, 1972.

Ludz, P.C., 'The SED leadership in transition', *Problems of Communism*, May–June 1970.

Ludz, P.C., 'Continuity and change since Ulbricht', *Problems of Communism*, March–April 1972.

Nagy, Imre, *Un Communisme qui n'oublie pas l'homme*, intro. by F. Fejto, Paris: Plon, 1957.

Narkiewicz, O.A., 'Polish or socialist?, *Universities Quarterly*, Brighton, September 1965.

Narkiewicz, O.A., *Marxism and the Reality of Power 1919–1980*, London: Croom Helm, 1981.

Narkiewicz, O.A., *Eastern Europe, 1968–86*, London and Sydney: Croom Helm, 1986.

Narkiewicz, O.A., *Soviet Leaders from the Cult of Personality to Collective Rule*, Brighton: Wheatsheaf, 1986.

Polonsky, A. and Drukier, B. (eds), *The Beginnings of Communist Rule in Poland*, London: Routledge and Kegan Paul, 1980.

Radio Free Europe, Munich, *Situation Reports* (Bulgaria, Czechoslovakia, Hungary, Romania).

Radio Free Europe, Munich, *Background Reports* (Czechoslovakia).

Ratiu, Ion, *Contemporary Romania: Her Place in World Affairs*, Richmond: Foreign Affairs Publishing Co., 1975.

Sandor, E., 'Hope and caution', *Problems of Communism*, January–February 1970.

Sanford, G., *Polish Communism in Crisis: The Politics of Reform and Reaction, 1980–81*, London: Croom Helm, 1983.

Shaffer, H.G., 'Progress in Hungary', *Problems of Communism*, January–February 1970.

Staar, R.F., 'Checklist of Communist parties in 1987', *Problems of Communism*, January–February 1988.

Stern, Carola, *Ulbricht: A political biography*, London: Pall Mall Press, 1965.

Suda, Zdenek L., *Zealots and Rebels: A History of the Communist Party of Czechoslovakia*, Stanford: Hoover University Press, 1980.

Taborsky, E., *Communism in Czechoslovakia, 1948–1960*, Princeton: Princeton University Press, 1961.

Tampke, Jürgen, *The People's Republics of Eastern Europe*, London: Croom Helm, 1983.
Tismaneanu, V., 'Ceausescu's socialism', *Problems of Communism*, January–February 1985.

Newspapers and journals consulted

Financial Times, London
International Herald Tribune, Paris
Le Monde, Paris
Neues Deutschland, East Berlin
New York Times, New York
The Observer, London
Polityka, Warsaw
Pravda, Moscow
Problems of Communism, Washington DC
Rude Pravo, Prague
The Sunday Times, London
Trybuna Ludu, Warsaw

Index